If These WALLS Could TALK:

DETROIT TIGERS

Stories from the Detroit Tigers Dugout, Locker Room, and Press Box

Mario Impemba with Mike Isenberg

TRIUMPH
B O O K S

Library of Congress Cataloging-in-Publication Data

Impemba, Mario.

If these walls could talk, Detroit Tigers : stories from the Detroit tigers dugout, locker room, and press box / Mario Impemba ; [foreword by] David Dombrowski.

pages cm

Summary: "Favorite stories and memories about the Detroit Tigers"— Provided by publisher.

Includes bibliographical references.

ISBN 978-1-60078-927-4 (pbk.)

1. Detroit Tigers (Baseball team)—History. 2. Detroit Tigers (Baseball team)—Anecdotes. I. Title.

GV875.D6I67 2014

796.357'640977434—dc23

2013050962

This book is available in quantity at special discounts for your group or organization. For further information, contact:

Triumph Books LLC
814 North Franklin Street
Chicago, Illinois 60610
(312) 337–0747
Fax (312) 280-5470
www.triumphbooks.com

Printed in U.S.A.

ISBN: 978-1-60078-927-4

Design by Amy Carter

To Andrew –

I Hope you Enjoy To Book!

Mario Impemba:

To Cathy, Brett, and Daniel. For all of the summers I spent away from home. For all of the missed games, concerts, and swim meets. For making my dream possible.

Mike Isenberg:

Covering sports is a privilege that I don't take lightly; not many people are lucky enough to work in the field they love. I dedicate this book to my two children, Zachary and Alexandra ("Cookie"). You guys are the reason I wake up each day, and know that you'll always be the top priority in my life.

CONTENTS

FOREWORD

You encounter numerous people working in the game of baseball for 35-plus years, and most have a common denominator in their passion and love for the game. Getting to know and work with Mario Impemba the past 12 seasons has been a true pleasure. You really get a feel for a person when you see and speak with them on a day-in, day-out basis and especially when traveling together on road trips. Mario is someone who appreciates the game and has a genuine affinity for its history, and in particular, the Detroit Tigers. Mario is a proud native Detroiter who grew up watching the Tigers play at old Tiger Stadium, idolizing stars like Alan Trammell, Jack Morris, and Lou Whitaker to name just a few.

Mario often admits his job is a dream job. He cherishes his role doing play-by-play for the Tigers for record-setting numbers of viewers on television. The Tigers have a rich broadcasting history, and Mario was fortunate to be mentored by the great Ernie Harwell. In fact, Mario's style, he will tell you, was shaped by listening to great Tigers announcers like Harwell, George Kell, and Paul Carey.

This book is an account of a local youngster who dreamed of following in Ernie Harwell's footsteps and into the Tigers broadcast booth. It features stories and experiences of how Mario certainly paid his dues, climbing the ladder from broadcasting in the minor leagues to a 20-year big league career.

Mario, like so many of us in baseball and sports, had to make sacrifices and go where the jobs were, and therefore spent his first seven seasons broadcasting for the Angels before returning home to Detroit in 2002 for his "dream job" as a Tigers announcer.

Mario has stood the test of time in his years with the Tigers. He demonstrated his professionalism and never wavered during the team's 119-loss season, to now enjoying the renaissance of Tigers baseball and its recent successes.

When you think of all the tradition, the Hall of Fame players and announcers this franchise has had representing the Olde English D, and you fast forward to the team's most recent success, you realize how entrenched Mario now is in Tigers history. He has forever carved his legacy, having described some of the greatest moments in Tigers history, including Miguel Cabrera's back-to-back MVPs and Triple Crown in 2012, two Justin Verlander no-hitters, and the list goes on. This book provides insight to Mario's wonderful story, and the beauty is that there are many more stories and chapters still to come.

— David Dombrowski
President, CEO, and General Manager
Detroit Tigers

ACKNOWLEDGMENTS

The authors would like to thank Al Kaline, Brayan Pena, Tim Kurkjian, Jim Leyland, David Dombrowski, Ernie Johnson, Prince Fielder, Miguel Cabrera, Ray Fosse, Torii Hunter, and all others who have shared their insights over the years.

I would also like to thank those who have given me the opportunity to carve out a career in baseball broadcasting, including Pete Vonachen, Mike Feder, John Savano, John Tuohey, the Los Angeles Angels, the Detroit Tigers, and all others who helped to further my career.

Thanks also to all of my colleagues in the game who have served as a sounding board over the years, including my broadcast partners Steve Quis, Bob Starr, Brian Barnhart, Daron Sutton, Rex Hudler, Kirk Gibson, and Rod Allen. A thank-you also to Tigers radio voice Dan Dickerson for his friendship and spending countless hours explaining WAR to me.

Finally, and most importantly, thanks to Dominic and Rose, parents who never questioned my decisions, but rather supported them.

—*Mario Impemba*

INTRODUCTION

Really, eight years in the minor leagues is not a very long time. For a player, yes, but not for a broadcaster.

You couldn't have convinced me of that back in 1994 when I was on the cusp of landing my first major league job with the Angels. I had just finished my eighth year of riding the buses and eating fast food every night. The lifestyle tends to wear you down. Then I hit the lottery. I was hired by a major league team.

It's somewhat strange to think that 27 years have passed since I first put on the headset in Peoria, Illinois, as a minor league broadcaster. The Peoria Chiefs versus the Springfield Cardinals was my first minor league broadcast in 1987. The only thing I can remember from that game is putting down the headsets at the end of a rain-filled night and thinking, *I've got 143 more of these to go?*

I wasn't sure this baseball thing was for me.

Now, as I embark on my 20th season broadcasting in the major leagues, I still can't believe I survived that first night in Peoria, let alone the fact that I showed up the next day.

I know how truly lucky I am. I can rattle off the names of dozens of announcers in the minor leagues who are still waiting for a chance to fulfill their dreams. They are no different from me. I am no more talented than them. I got lucky. They haven't yet.

I've done everything from pulling the tarp and pushing the broken-down team bus in the minors to covering multiple World Series in Detroit. I've met and worked with personal broadcasting idols like Ernie Harwell, Paul Carey, and Vin Scully, as well as on-field heroes like Al Kaline, Alan Trammell, and Willie Horton. I often wonder why I was given this chance.

Detroit is a city rich in broadcasting talent. Every major sport in this town has produced some of its game's best broadcasters. To work among them is a dream.

Broadcasting games into a recorder on your couch in Sterling Heights, Michigan, as a kid seems like a long way from the television booth at Comerica Park. In reality, it's not. Aspiring broadcasters need to realize that if I can do it, so can they. With hard work and a dash of luck, anything is doable.

This is a book about some of my experiences. Good or bad, they were all worthwhile.

This I do know—getting a chance to broadcast Major League Baseball in your home town is something I wish every broadcaster could experience.

It really has been a fascinating ride.

CHAPTER 1
THE MINORS:
PAYING MY DUES

Pass the Toilet Paper

Like baseball players, most baseball announcers spend time in the minor leagues, honing their skills and hoping for a shot at the big leagues.

Even with that goal in mind, I wouldn't trade one minute of my minor league experience. Where I'm now fortunate enough to travel on team charters and stay at five-star hotels, that wasn't always the case. Working in the minor leagues will keep you humble and give you important perspective. It will also teach you how to be resourceful.

In 1987, I was broadcasting for the Peoria Chiefs, the Class A affiliate of the Chicago Cubs. I was 24 years old and just two years out of college. This was my second job.

The team had just completed a three-game series in Wausau, Wisconsin, with a trip to Appleton awaiting us.

In the minor leagues, broadcasting is often a one-man job. I was serving as announcer, engineer, analyst, and the guy who set up and broke down equipment before and after games. Eventually, it all becomes routine, which is good. If the announcer isn't five minutes early for the bus, he's late, and the team ain't waiting.

On this day, I was running a little behind but was able to make the bus. For some reason, though, I felt out of sorts. I figured it was just the adrenaline of the game and rushing to board.

Two hours went by, and we pulled into the hotel in Appleton. My uneasiness was about to go into full-fledged panic.

The trainer unloaded the bus, and my suitcase was one of the first off (since I was one of the last to board). I waited patiently for my equipment case...and waited...and waited.

When the final bag was pulled off the bus, I finally figured out why I had that strange feeling. I had left the equipment case back in Wausau, two hours away!

It was now 11:00 AM, about eight hours before game time. This was not good. The game was going to start at 7:00 PM, with or without me. And if I wasn't on the air, I would have a hard time explaining to my boss why. My broadcasting career, as it was, flashed before my eyes.

As cutthroat as broadcasting can be, we all realize that at some point, we are going to need help. Maybe a machine breaks down, or we need information about a player on the other team. Or some schmuck leaves his equipment behind. Usually, we try to help our colleagues. Thankfully, this was a lesson I was about to learn.

I called a local radio station and explained my predicament. Our bus driver took me to the station, and they were kind enough to lend me enough equipment to save the broadcast (and possibly my hide).

Now beggars can't be choosers, but when I got to the ballpark, I realized that this was really bare-bones equipment, with just enough to pull off the show. There was no headset—just a mixer board and microphone with no stand. To do this game, I was going to have to hold the mic non-stop for three hours.

This is the resourcefulness I mentioned. How could I do the game while having to hold the mic the entire time? After all, I need to keep my scorebook, take notes, and cue up highlights for the postgame show. That's not easy to do with one hand occupied.

One thing that minor league parks do have is a restroom. So I went inside and lifted a roll of toilet paper. I taped the roll of toilet paper to the counter and jammed the mic into the cardboard roll.

This is ridiculous, I thought. Was I really going to sit in the middle of the press box with my mic jammed into a roll of Charmin?

The answer was yes.

That night, I broadcasted an entire minor league baseball game with my microphone sticking out of a roll of toilet paper.

Since it was radio, and cell phones with cameras hadn't been invented yet, there would be no proof—until a fan sitting just in front of me aimed her camera at me and snapped a picture of me talking into a roll of two-ply.

So somewhere in Appleton, Wisconsin, exists a photo of a young broadcaster calling a professional baseball game into a roll of toilet paper, which was a heck of a lot better than a young broadcaster watching his career go down the toilet.

Initiation

It's one of baseball's oldest traditions, and it's not peanuts and cracker jacks or keeping score of the game in your program. It's bigger than that. I'm talking about the practical joke. The old hot foot, shaving cream in the cap, Ben-Gay in the athletic supporter kind of joke. Nobody is safe—not the best player, not the worst player, not even the manager. And as I learned, not even the play-by-play announcer.

The good news is that for an announcer, being the target of a practical joke is a sign that the guys on the team like you and it makes you feel like you belong. During the 1993 season, I learned that I really belonged.

It was my seventh year in the business broadcasting AAA baseball in Tucson, Arizona, for the Astros. On any AAA team, you have two types of players. One is the young guy on the verge of a major league opportunity. Future All-Star closer Todd Jones would be called up later that season. The second is a veteran player who is trying to make his way back to the big leagues. Perhaps he's been injured, or maybe he's just lost his skills and is working for one more shot.

An example of a guy looking for one more shot on this team was Jim Lindeman. Jim came into the game as a first-round draft pick of the St. Louis Cardinals. Now he was a 31-year-old journeyman. Seven years earlier, Lindeman had his best year in the minors with 20 home runs and 96 RBI. That earned him a call-up with the Cardinals. He also played with the Tigers and Phillies.

Now he was just another guy, hoping for one last shot. The reason an organization would sign Lindeman was to hopefully catch lightning in a bottle but also to add depth to the organization or try to set the tone with their young players.

One night before a game I was hanging around the cage watching early batting practice when one of the guys invited me to take a few hacks. They didn't need to ask me twice. This was like fantasy camp except better. I played some ball in high school, but I was only a bench player. Stepping into a cage on a professional diamond was nirvana for me.

This was my big chance. Many players look at announcers as wannabes who never had the skill to compete. This was an opportunity to show that I had some ability—and in some small way to show that I belonged in their world.

I was told to grab the bat leaning against the cage. I looked down, and it had Lindeman's name etched on it. Someone told me it was just his batting practice bat.

The first pitch came. Swing and a miss. Second pitch, and I hit a soft line drive to center field. I had my first base hit—but it came at a price.

You've heard the phrase "crack of the bat," right? Well, I cracked it okay. Actually, I cracked the bat! I was a little uneasy—this wasn't my bat—but I didn't think it was a big deal.

As I walked out of the cage, Jim Lindeman came running out of the dugout screaming, "Did you break my bat?"

I replied with a meek, "Umm, yeah."

"That was my gamer. You broke my game bat! I can't believe you broke my game bat! Why would you even touch my bat?"

If you've been around the game long enough, you learn to understand the relationship players have with their equipment. With certain guys, you just don't touch their bats or gloves. It's sacrosanct. You can do a high five with their kids, tap them on the shoulder, but *do not touch* their bats or gloves. I had figured since this was only his BP bat, it wasn't a big deal. Clearly, I was wrong, and now Lindeman was about to snap me in half. I was freaking out.

As Lindeman approached me, the team started laughing. I had been had. The bat already had a hairline fracture in it and all it took was any contact to finish the job.

The score that night was Players 1, Me 0. They had set me up and nailed me perfectly. After a good laugh, my heart rate returned to normal and I was assured Jim Lindeman was in on the whole thing and had no intention of throttling me. Now I just had to return my blood pressure to normal levels and call the game.

Nice Effort!

Most baseball announcers at one time dreamed of playing professionally. Most realize that isn't going to happen, so the next step is the booth. Following my ill-fated attempt at batting practice with a busted bat, I got another opportunity to show off my skills.

We were on the road one night in 1993, playing a game in Portland, Oregon.

Minor league teams didn't typically carry the volume of coaches that a big-league team does. At that time it was just a manager and a pitching coach.

That night in Portland I finished my game prep early, so I was hanging around the field as the team prepared to take infield practice. The crowd was filing into the ballpark, settling into their seats, and I decided to head back to the booth to get ready for the broadcast.

As I was leaving the field, our pitching coach Brent Strom called me over and asked if I could do him a big favor.

"Sure. What is it?"

It appeared the team was going to take infield that night but Strom had a pitchers scouting meeting scheduled. The manager was busy so there was no one to hit fungos (ground balls) to the infielders. Strom asked if I think I could do it.

"Sure, I'd love to."

"Keep it simple," Strom said. "Go around the infield third to first and just hit ground balls. Nothing fancy."

"No problem."

As soon as he handed me the fungo bat, I instantly turned into a nervous, uncoordinated non-athlete. While I never played beyond high school, I was a good athlete and decent player. But not on this night.

As I aimed toward third to hit my first grounder, the ball flared off my bat and ended up in short right field. Great. I missed my target by about 180'.

I tried it again, and my second attempt ended up behind home plate against the screen. With that, Strom walked back from his scouting meeting and took the bat from me.

"Well, that went well," he said.

And with that, he scrapped his meeting and hit infield.

As I walked back to the booth embarrassed, a fan in the first couple of rows yelled out to me, "Nice effort!"

"Shut up!" I yelled back.

I remember thinking, *Shut up? That's all you could think of?*

The worst part was that the broadcast area was located right behind home plate, at field level, next to the fans. They nicknamed me "Fungo," and I heard from them all night.

Within the span of two swings, I had proven why most play-by-play guys belong in the booth.

I'm Not Terry Clark

One of the great things about minor league baseball is intimacy. Back in the 1950s, when baseball was a part-time job, fans could walk into a store and see their favorite player working behind the counter. They might even be your neighbor. Willie Mays, for example, was well-known for playing stickball with kids on the streets of Brooklyn.

These days, with the average major league salary in excess of $3 million, there aren't too many players holding offseason jobs. But the affection from fans hasn't wavered much.

When we're on the road, I see two types of fans. The first is the old-school fan. Of course, this includes kids, who are just thrilled to get a signature on a baseball or even a notebook. I remember being this type of fan, sending letters to the team and asking for autographs.

The other fan is the collector. One of the unfortunate aspects of baseball is exactly how big collecting has become. Don't get me wrong—it's great that there's a passion for the game. But to some people, it's just a business. They show up with a book full of 15 cards for each player and want to get each one signed. It doesn't matter whether he's the best player on the team or the 25th man on the roster. They just want to get the signature. That's a shame.

In 1991, while I was broadcasting for the Tucson Toros, one of our players was a journeyman pitcher named Terry Clark. Clark was the prototypical Crash Davis from *Bull Durham*. This guy was perseverance personified. He played for *17* different minor league teams. Once he got to the majors, he played for the Angels, Astros, Braves, Orioles, the Royals, the Astros again, Indians, and Rangers.

Back in '91, Terry was toiling in Tucson, trying to make it back to the major leagues. By this time, he had won 81 games in the minor leagues, which is pretty impressive. It's also 81 more wins than I had recorded. But one night in Tacoma, Washington, none of this mattered.

I had decided to get to the ballpark early that night because I had to secure and conduct several interviews. To give me time to set up, I took a taxi instead of waiting for the team bus. That's where the trouble began.

Whenever a cab pulls up to the ballpark, fans will immediately swarm around it. Most of them have baseball cards ready to be signed. I figured, "Hey, I'm a AAA announcer. I'll be fine." I was dramatically wrong.

Most of the time when I get out of a taxi, the fans feel they're seeing a wet towel being thrown on a fire. I can hear it almost every time.

"It's not a player. He's a no one."

Things are a little different now. With Tigers fans all over the country, I feel fortunate that they show me their appreciation wherever we are. But back in my AAA days, that wasn't the case.

So we're in Tacoma, and I get out of the cab. A man and his son thought I was Terry Clark. On this day, let's say Terry was pretty lucky. The guy and his son approached me.

"Mr. Clark, would you sign this for my son?"

A couple of problems here. First, it was obvious to me that he was using his kid to get an autograph. Then there was also the other problem. I was not Terry Clark.

Let's examine the tale of the tape:

	Terry Clark	Me
Height	6'2"	5'10"
Weight	190	160
Hair	Full head of black	Not so much

I politely informed the man that I was not Clark and didn't want to sign the baseball card. But that was not good enough.

The man became irate. He swore at me several times in front of his son and accused me of being a spoiled athlete.

"Sir, I can't sign that card. I'm not Terry Clark," I said.

He refused to believe me and continued to follow me toward the stadium gate.

Fearing this guy was a little unstable, I turned toward him and signed the card.

The father had taught his boy a lesson. "See, son? You can't take no for an answer," he proudly boasted.

The real lesson in the story, however, is this. If you're ever in a Tacoma card shop and see a Terry Clark autographed baseball card, save your money!

That's Not What I Said

Have you ever played the game Telephone? One person tells a story to another, and it goes around the room a few times. It's amazing by the end how the story is nothing like what was originally said.

Broadcasting is like Telephone. All announcers will tell you that before your career is over, you will be misunderstood. Words will be put in your mouth, and selective hearing is your worst enemy.

I found this out early in my career while broadcasting in the minor leagues. Players obviously can't listen to the broadcast because they are on the field, but family and friends sure do, and in most cases they are not bashful about telling players what the announcers are saying about them, especially when they perceive it as being negative.

Most times it is pretty accurate, but many times it is not.

When I was broadcasting in A ball early in my career, I noticed I was getting the cold shoulder from a lot of players and coaches. I made my rounds in the clubhouse before a game, and the players were avoiding me like the plague. No one was talking to me, and I didn't understand what was going on. Finally, one of the players filled me in.

"Skip told us not to talk to you or do any interviews," he said.

"What? Why?"

"Something about you interviewing one of the other team's players."

I approached the manager later that day and asked what was going on.

"My wife heard your pregame show last night. She said you interviewed Ty Griffin and were talking up the other team."

"Well, Ty Griffin was the Cubs' No. 1 pick in the draft. Why wouldn't I interview him?"

"He's one of their players. You broadcast for us. Besides, she said it sounded like you were rooting for them."

"Okay, yeah, that's it. I want us to lose. It's much more fun to broadcast a loser."

Yes, I did interview an opposing player on the pre-game show. The truth is, I had already talked to all of our players repeatedly and was just trying to get a different perspective. And keep it fresh.

As far as favoring the opponent, I simply ask, "What's the benefit for me?" These days, I cover the Tigers. Do I want the Tigers to win? Of course! Not just because I'm a Michigander, but my job is a lot easier and more fun when the team I'm covering wins.

Another incident took place when I was broadcasting for Tucson. We had just finished up a game in Colorado Springs, and our starting pitcher was shelled that night. As I wrapped up the game on the postgame show, I stated that our starting pitcher just didn't have it that night and I repeated his final totals.

The next day he wouldn't speak to me because he said his wife told him I was trashing him on the air. It was another case of selective hearing. I simply recapped his numbers and moved on. It is my job to let fans know what happened in the game. In this case, I was really just giving the facts, not interpreting them.

Most players understand your job is to report what happens on the field. And I will admit there are some announcers who will not pass up a chance to pile on a player if he is struggling.

That, however, is not my style and won't ever be. I never played professionally and have no idea what it takes to compete at that level. If an analyst wants to sharply criticize someone, chances are he's a former player, so I think that's a little bit different. But my job is to tell the fans what's going on. In fact, I've even had players tell me that I need to be more honest and stop protecting players so much.

I have learned to make sure I say what I mean and be ready for someone to hear it differently.

CHAPTER 2
CLIMBING THE LADDER

Can I Really Do This?

Ever since I was a kid, I wanted to be a major league announcer. I also wanted to play center field for the Tigers. But just because you want it doesn't mean you can do it.

I enrolled at Michigan State University with the determined goal of becoming a broadcaster, either in Major League Baseball or NBA basketball. But I almost didn't even make it through college.

I was fortunate to get a job at the campus radio station at MSU through the kindness (foolishness) of Dave Dye. Dave wrote for the *Detroit News* from 1985 to 2009. He currently writes for foxsportsdetroit.com. During my freshman year in college, Dave was the sports director for the campus station. The opportunity gave me a chance to cut my teeth doing play-by-play for the Spartans baseball, basketball, and hockey teams.

My first play-by-play opportunity came as a freshman when I was given a women's basketball game to call between Michigan State and Purdue. I was *not* going to let this opportunity slip away.

I prepped like a mad man for the game, and within a few minutes, it was clear that I was overmatched. The pace was furious, I was ultra nervous, and I misidentified one player after another. The broadcast was the worst piece of radio in the medium's history.

After the disaster, I went back to my dorm room and curled up into the fetal position the rest of the night. How could I possibly be this bad? I learned that night that calling a game on my couch is vastly different than the real thing.

Going in, I knew I had some work to do, but this felt like I had just learned the English language. I was shocked that I had failed so miserably. All the prep and all the desire couldn't keep me from bombing. I decided that night to change my major and pursue something else. I had no idea what major that would be, but it sure as heck wasn't going to be broadcasting.

This was when I learned the value of perspective. After a restless night of sleep, I woke up the next day and decided I would give it another shot—provided, of course, that the station would give me another shot.

My next opportunity was a Big 10 baseball game. My determination was high. I would use the failure of my first chance as motivation to improve. Maybe it was a little bit better, but I struggled again.

For whatever reason, though, I gained some determination. However long this took, I was committed to doing it. Sure enough, with each game I got better and better. There were definitely more growing pains—and after nearly 20 years covering baseball, there still are. I try and learn something each game and try to get better. You can't stop trying to learn because the business is always evolving.

When I talk to young kids, I emphasize that Rome wasn't built in a day. There's a reason that everyone covets these jobs—it's because they're hard to get! And I'm living proof. My career nearly ended before it ever got off the ground.

You Can't Do It Alone

To achieve success in any field, everyone needs some help along the way. Miguel Cabrera and Justin Verlander get all the headlines, but without the Tigers training and support staff, those guys don't even get on the field.

Television and radio is no different. Viewers at home get to see and hear me doing something I love, but believe me, it takes a village. Without a lot of help, I would never even be on the air.

When I arrived at Michigan State University in 1981, it wouldn't be a stretch to say I was overwhelmed. For reasons only known to him, MSU radio sports director Dave Dye gave me my first chance in "the business." While I eventually worked my way up the ladder, my first assignment was the fencing beat. Seriously—fencing. Who knew there was a fencing beat?

People talk about different skills that are needed in this business, such as work ethic, creativity, and desire. But one of the most critical skills is networking. As the old saying goes, it's not what you know but who you know.

Matt McConnell was a roommate of mine at MSU. He is one of my best friends in broadcasting. Matt has forged his career in the NHL as the voice of the Anaheim Ducks, Pittsburgh Penguins, Atlanta Thrashers, Minnesota Wild, and now the Phoenix Coyotes.

Back in 1986, Matt was working minor league hockey in Peoria, Illinois, when he alerted me of an opening with the Peoria Chiefs, the minor league baseball team in town.

Matt was looking out for me because he knew I was looking for a job at the time, and I will always be thankful. He helped open the door that got me started on my path up the baseball ladder.

Another critical ingredient in any business is loyalty. Whenever someone has helped me out or given me a break, it makes me want to run through a wall for him.

Mike Feder first gave me a job with the Quad City Angels of the Midwest League in 1989. Three years later, he took over as the General Manager of the AAA Tucson Toros and hired me there. Mike had always been one of my biggest supporters, and this was a great opportunity for me to jump from A ball to AAA—just one step away from the majors. Again, if he hadn't given me this chance, I likely would not have gotten my shot in the majors.

I finally got that first big-league job in 1995 when John Sevano, the director of broadcasting for the Angels, took a chance on a hungry guy working in the minors. California (as they were then known) was a great job, and there was no shortage of candidates. The safe play was to hire someone who was already working in the big leagues or had major-market experience. I'm not sure what convinced John to take a chance on me, but I'll never forget his vote of confidence.

Sometimes all it takes is for one person to believe in you. The confidence that belief inspires often makes the difference in reaching your dreams.

CHAPTER 3
CALIFORNIA DREAMIN'

Not Getting On That Cruz

With a last name like Impemba—pronounced "Im-PEM-bah"—I've come to expect just about every pronunciation but the correct one. I've been called everything from Mario Amoeba to Mario Impala. Those interpretations would come in handy if I were a shapeless organism or a Chevy.

I figured it wouldn't be that hard to say my name. I mean, my job is partly based on saying other people's names correctly. Is it "Oc-TAH-vio" or "Oc-TAY-vio" Dotel? Is it "PLA-cee-do" or "Pla-CEE-do" Polanco?

And it's not like these are insignificant details, either. Guys want to have their names pronounced correctly. It's a pretty common courtesy.

Because of that reason, I've always been very sensitive to trying to get it right. I've also been sensitive to the difficulty people have while pronouncing my last name. Personally, I don't think it should be so hard—I've never had trouble with it—but for many people, it's been a challenge. Because of that, I've often thought about changing it for professional reasons and for simplicity. However, it is my name, and I've decided not to change it.

In fact, when I got my first big-league job, it was suggested that I do just that. I remember back in 1994, I was in Los Angeles interviewing for the Angels radio job. I was sitting in the executive offices of the radio station that was doing the hiring, and as the interview was winding down, the program director had one last question. "You're Hispanic, right?"

"Umm, no, I'm Italian," I replied. "Does that make a difference?" I asked, a little bit surprised because you really can't ask that question during an interview.

"Not really. It's just that we have a large Hispanic population here in Southern California, and your last name is difficult to pronounce," he said. "If you were to change it, it might be best."

"What do you have in mind?" I asked.

"How about Mario Cruz?"

I thought to myself, *How about no?* Mario Cruz? How about Tom Cruise? Don't get me wrong, I desperately wanted my shot at the Majors. This, however, was over the line. Not only do I have to change my last name, but apparently I have to change my heritage, too. I thought about how disappointed my mother and father would be if I changed my last name.

Jobs come and go, but your family is always there, so I rolled the dice and said that I preferred not to change it. At that point, I thought it might be a deal breaker.

I ended up getting the job, and the folks of Southern California learned to pronounce it correctly.

Fast-forward to my first spring training with the Angels in 1995. I remember picking up my first major league credential. Every season, announcers and other media members get a credential, a pass that gets them into all of the games. It's something that all aspiring broadcasters dream about—your first big league credential. Even today, when I get my season credential, it's still a cool moment, kind of like the first day of school.

So here I was, getting one for the first time. I had finally made it. I picked up the credential, saw my photo, and stared at my name in big letters: Marlo Impemba!

Really? They got the Impemba part right, but misspelled Mario? But it's moments like this that can make a memory. Even today, nearly 20 years later, my Angels friends still call me Marlo.

Even when people mean well, I still get a variety of names. Probably the most common is mispronouncing my first name. When people ask me, I say my name is "Mah-rio." That doesn't stop a lot of people from calling me "Meh-rio." Oh, well. Believe it or not, some fans even see me at the park and yell, "Hey Rod, what's up?" All you can do is laugh.

When you think about it, names have been a huge part of baseball history. There have been plenty of unusual names in baseball, such as Boots Day, Razor Shines, Tim Spooneybarger, Boof Bonser, Tuffy Rhodes, Pickles Dillhoefer, Biff Pocoroba, Van Lingle Mungo, and Bombo Rivera.

Come to think of it, Pickles Impemba has a nice ring to it.

My First Time

If you ask most ballplayers about their first game, they'll be able to tell you everything about it—the opponent, the situation when they came up to bat, or the moment they took the mound for the first time. Most players remember it like it was yesterday. Of course, some guys don't remember a single thing. It's like they weren't even there.

For broadcasters, everyone remembers his or her first game. My first major league broadcast was on April 26, 1995. Remember, the 1995 season was shortened as the result of the 1994 strike, which canceled the World Series for the first time. The players were pumped up, and so was I.

Ironically, the team that hired me (the Angels) were facing the team that I grew up rooting for—the Detroit Tigers. Chuck Finley started against Mike Moore. The Tigers led in the eighth when Cecil Fielder clobbered a two-run homer for a three-run lead, the bullpen held off an Angels rally, and the Tigers won 5–4. One of my coolest memories that day was walking into the Tigers clubhouse and seeing Kirk Gibson, Alan Trammell, and a lot of the Tigers I had rooted for. I also interviewed Sparky Anderson for our pregame show. It couldn't have been scripted any better.

Of course, there is one other thing I remember about that game. It was probably the most nervous I'd ever been.

It wasn't like I hadn't paid my dues. I spent eight seasons in the minor leagues and had more than 1,000 games under my belt. I kept telling myself that baseball is baseball, the game is the same, and I was ready. But there was no question about it—this was *not* just another game.

Just like a rookie player, I had finally made the big show. No more long bus rides to Wausau, Wisconsin, or Burlington, Iowa. This was the Big Leagues!

As much as I told myself I was ready, there was definitely a little part of me wondering if that was true. Now, instead of a few hundred listeners, there would be thousands. That's considerably more pressure.

Yet when I took the mic for the middle three innings and Rudy Pemberton doubled off Chuck Finley to start the fourth inning, it was just like any other game. I only wished my first batter as a big league broadcaster would have been Cecil Fielder or Alan Trammell or Kirk Gibson. Instead, I got Rudy Pemberton.

Thankfully, my big-league debut went smoothly, but as I've learned, those nerves never completely go away. Every year, the first telecast, even in spring training, is a challenge. I always do my research, but did I do enough? Am I up to speed on all of the new players, the new storylines? It's almost like I have to prove to myself that I can still do this every spring. My guess is that when I stop getting excited about it, that's when it's time to walk away.

Rudy Pemberton? Really?

There's nothing like your first time. Ask any player—or in my case, any broadcaster—about their first game. My debut was April 26, 1995, with the California Angels. It was going to be special, no matter what. The fact that the Angels were hosting my hometown team, the Tigers, made it an unlikely debut but exciting nonetheless.

I arrived at the ballpark at 2:30 PM for the 7:30 game. Of course I was excited, but I was so nervous that I nearly got sick. We were just hours away from my first game, and it was against my favorite team. That's a pretty good start.

My first step was the standard manager interview. Except this was nothing standard. This was future Hall of Famer Sparky Anderson.

For Sparky, it didn't matter if it was Vin Scully or little Mario Impemba. He was generous with his time and answered all of my questions. Walking out of his office, I remember thinking, *I can't believe Sparky Anderson just gave me an interview.* It was difficult to maintain a professional attitude while walking through the Tigers clubhouse.

As I walked into the locker room. I instantly reverted to my childhood (at least in my mind). They were all there—Alan Trammell, Kirk Gibson, Lou Whitaker, and Cecil Fielder, sitting at their lockers. Yes, I had questions, but I just couldn't pull the trigger. I was too intimidated to talk to any of them.

So I headed up to the press box dining room. I was even more awestruck. One of the greatest broadcasting teams of all time—George Kell and Ernie Harwell—was eating just a few feet from me. Two Hall of Famers. And just like in the clubhouse, I was too intimidated to introduce myself. To this day, it's one of my biggest regrets. While I was fortunate enough to become friends with Ernie, this would turn out to be my only chance to meet George.

Now that I had missed these two golden opportunities, it was time for the game. The Tigers rode home runs by Cecil Fielder and Juan Samuel to a 5–4 victory.

Part of my postgame duties was to conduct the postgame interview. One of our interns was in charge of setting up the interview as the players walked off the field. The player would put on a headset, and I would ask the questions from the booth.

I really had no say as to which player would be selected, but there were plenty of big names to choose from. But who did I get? Someone named Rudy Pemberton.

Sure, he had gone 3-for-4, but Rudy Pemberton?

I turned to my partner Bob Starr and said, "What in the world do I ask Rudy Pemberton?"

Bob turned to me and said, "Welcome to the big leagues, young man. How's your Spanish?"

Rudy's answer to my first three questions was, "Thank you. We play good today."

You see, Rudy didn't speak English.

Awesome.

My first big-league interview would be with a player that would go on to play a grand total of 52 games in the major leagues. While he seemed like a pleasant fellow, it may have been the worst interview I ever conducted.

It didn't matter, though. My first game was in the books.

Colossal Collapse

As I worked my way through my first season as a big-league announcer, I had the great fortune of announcing for a team that was having a lot of success.

By the second week of August, the Angels team was on its way to the playoffs with a record of 60–36. There were stars everywhere, including Tim Salmon, Garret Anderson, and Jim Edmonds, and their lead in the American League West was a whopping 11 games.

In all, this roster had featured ten players who would make the All-Star team. They also had a secret weapon—their play-by-play announcer.

I was on a roll. In my last five minor league seasons, three of the teams I covered won championships. Clearly, I was on my way to another.

Gary DiSarcina of the Anaheim Angels during a game at Anaheim Stadium in Anaheim, California, during the 1997 season. *(Larry Goren/Four Seam Images via AP Images)*

One of the things I've come to learn about baseball is its unpredictability. On this team of stars, it was an injury to an unsung player that had the most impact on one of baseball's all-time collapses.

By just about any objective measure, shortstop Gary DiSarcina was a solid player. His lifetime batting average was a pedestrian .258. (In fact, 1995 was one of only two full seasons in which he hit higher than .260). He never had more than five home runs, and he was a good defender. Yet for some reason, on this team of stars, DiSarcina was the glue that held everything together. As I look back, his grit made him one of my favorite players to cover.

As I look back on the collapse of the 1995 Angels, it's easy to pick the turning point. If you look up August 3, you'll see that the Halos lost to Seattle. But the defeat was much more costly than the one game in the standings.

In the bottom of the seventh inning, the Mariners led 10–2, but these Angels never felt like they were out of a game. DiSarcina singled to center. Maybe he was trying to start a rally, or maybe he was just playing hard as usual, but on a ground ball to second, Gary plowed into shortstop Alex Rodriguez while trying to break up a double play. The result was torn ligaments in his thumb. That night everything changed, and I'm not talking about the 10–7 score.

J.T. Snow called DiSarcina the heart and soul of the team, and Snow proved to be 100 percent right. During the next 40 games, the Angels went 16–24. The season was spiraling out of control. In late August, they went on a nine-game losing streak.

By the middle of September the lead had shrunk to four games. I hosted a postgame talk show following every broadcast that season, and the natives were getting restless. It was my job to talk them off the ledge, but the truth is, I was ready to jump off, too. The ship was sinking, and the pressure was mounting.

After taking two out of three against the White Sox, we thought perhaps things were back on track.

Until they went on another nine-game slide.

On September 20 in Oakland, the Halos battled back from a 9–0 ninth-inning deficit only to lose 9–6. Meanwhile, in Seattle, the Mariners were busy pounding Texas 11–3 behind a career day by utility player Luis Sojo, who had six RBI.

The 11-game lead was gone. All of it.

The Mariners had somehow caught the Angels and were tied for first place with nine games to play. I remember the look of shock on everyone's face, from manager Marcel Lachemann to first-base coach Joe Maddon. The unthinkable had now happened, firmly placing the Angels on the cusp of baseball history.

When experts talk about the biggest collapses of all time, the 1978 Red Sox are usually the first team mentioned. That team blew a 14-game lead over the hated New York Yankees. What people don't remember is that Boston had to win their last eight games to force a one-game playoff. (Just ask any Red Sox fan about Bucky "bleeping" Dent.)

Similarly, the Angels didn't go down without a fight. But not even DiSarcina's return was enough to stem that second nine-game losing streak, which left them two games out of first. They had every reason to pack it in. But then something strange happened.

First, Chuck Finley shut down Seattle 2–0.

Then Mark Langston did the same to Oakland 4–1.

Next, "Wonder Dog" Rex Hudler went 4–4 in a 9–6 win over the A's.

J.T. Snow, Jim Edmonds, Rex Hudler, and Chili Davis both went deep on Saturday night in a 9–3 win, and when Seattle lost at Texas, the Angels were back within one game of first place with one game to play.

On the last day of the regular season, Kenny Rogers and the Rangers beat Seattle 9–3, and the Angels had their chance.

Finley was dominant, striking out nine Athletics in 7⅓ innings. When Troy Percival struck out Scott Brosius to end the game, the Angels had an 8–2 win and forced a one-game playoff with the Mariners for the division title.

In the event the Angels would win on the final day, we had packed our bags and brought them to the ballpark just in case we would be traveling to Seattle. Even after blowing an 11-game lead, the fans still believed.

We normally would board the team busses behind the stadium, but that day they pulled the buses to the front of the ballpark, and walking through the front gates of the stadium was an unforgettable experience, with thousands of fans cheering. Yes, they were cheering for the players, but it was a great experience to be part of.

Congratulations! Now Go Beat Randy

In 20 years of broadcasting baseball, I've seen some of the all-time greats, including Roger Clemens, Greg Maddux, and Pedro Martinez. But there's no question who was the most dominant. And there's also no question about the day he was most dominant.

After a historic collapse, the Angels had fought to force a one-game playoff with the Mariners. With five straight wins to close the season, the Angels were feeling pretty good about themselves. Mark Langston, who had won 15 games that season, was on the hill with a chance to get the team into the postseason.

Now, Langston was a very good pitcher—a four-time All-Star. But on October 2, 1995, I think Cy Young himself could have been on the mound and it wouldn't have made a difference.

When Randy Johnson broke into the majors with Montreal in 1988, he was power personified. He could easily throw in the high 90s, but he didn't always know where the ball was going to go. He was a 6'10" lefty, so when the ball left his hand, it seemed as if it was already at home plate.

In his second year with the Expos, Johnson was traded to Seattle—for Mark Langston, ironically. With the Mariners, Johnson was still a little bit out of control. In his first three full seasons with the Mariners, Johnson had a 39–35 record, and he led the American League in walks each year. (He led the AL in strikeouts in his third season, as well.)

Then something clicked, and baseball history would never be the same. The Big Unit led the league in strikeouts for each of the next three seasons. But with better control, he went 50–16.

Major league hitters don't usually fear anyone. They may not be able to hit a certain pitcher, but it's not like they're scared when they step to the plate. Between his height, velocity, and what became "controlled wildness," many players feared Randy Johnson. I had several players over the years admit to me they hoped for a day off when Randy pitched.

In 1995, Johnson came into that one-game playoff with a 17–2 record. He was on his way to his first Cy Young Award, and he led the league in ERA. With Johnson's blistering fastball and unhittable slider, the Angels were up against it. The combination of an untouchable Johnson and a super-charged Kingdome crowd, hungry for their first postseason appearance, would set up the most dominant performance by a left hander I've ever seen.

The first four innings were intense. Langston was pitching well, scattering four meaningless singles and no runs. Johnson, on the other hand, was ridiculous, recording nine strikeouts without giving up a hit. He struck out the side both in the third and fifth innings. With each pitch, it seemed that the 52,000 Mariner fans got louder and louder. We couldn't even hear ourselves during the broadcast.

I asked our engineer, Kirt Daniels, if he could help.

"Kirt, I can't hear myself. Can you turn down the crowd mic?"

"I killed the crowd mic. All of the noise is coming through your headset mic," he said.

It was the loudest crowd I had ever experienced during a sporting event.

The crowd only became louder when the Mariners blew open a tight game with four runs in the seventh on a three-run double by Luis Sojo and four more runs in the eighth. The only thing left to decide was the final score and Johnson's final numbers. But this was no fair fight. Johnson looked like he was throwing to little leaguers—that's how dominant he looked. The Big Unit threw a complete game three-hitter with 12 strikeouts. The final score was Mariners 9, Angels 1. If possible, the game wasn't even that close.

I had just witnessed the most dominating performance from the most dominating pitcher I had ever seen in the big leagues.

Technically, we had made the postseason, so my streak of bringing a club good luck continued, at least for one more day.

My luck with the Angels really ran out a few years later when, after leaving Anaheim for Detroit in 2002, the Halos won the World Series. I guess maybe I wasn't the good luck charm after all.

Incoming!

There are certain moments that define a player's career. What people don't always take into account is that there's always someone on the other side of that moment, and it can affect them just as much.

For example, Mookie Wilson hits a dribbler down the first-base line, but it's Bill Buckner, a much better player than Wilson, that everyone remembers because the ball went through his legs.

We've seen it in Detroit, as well, when Magglio Ordonez hit the three-run homer to put the Tigers into the 2006 World Series. Huston Street was the defending Rookie of the Year and put up 37 saves in that 2006 season. He gave up the shot to Maggs and has only had one season that even came close to that number. He's never been the same.

One of the most famous home runs of all time came in 1993 when Joe Carter won the World Series for Toronto with his ninth-inning, three-run home run off of Phillies reliever Mitch Williams.

It's easy to forget that 1993 was actually the best season of Williams' career. If not for the "Wild Thing" and his long-flowing mullet, the Phils never would have made it to the postseason. That year the Phillies recorded 46 saves. Williams accounted for 43 of them.

Philadelphia may be known as the City of Brotherly Love, but the Phillies front office knew that it would be nearly impossible for the eccentric lefty to return the following season, so they traded Williams to Houston.

From there, the end came pretty quickly. Williams posted a 7.65 ERA in 25 games with the Astros and was released by the end of May.

But in baseball, if you throw left handed and have a pulse, you're going to get more chances. Sure enough, during the strike of 1994, Wild Thing signed with the California Angels. As luck would have it, 1995 would also be my first season in the big leagues.

The '95 Angels actually had a very good bullpen. Lee Smith, who retired as the all-time saves leader, had also signed as a free agent. Troy Percival, who became the Angels career saves leader, was a rookie on the team. If Williams would ever regain his confidence, this seemed like a good, low-pressure opportunity.

Unfortunately for Mitch, he was basically finished as an effective major leaguer. After holding the opposition scoreless in 10 of his first 12 appearances, things unraveled, and they unraveled quickly.

On May 26, the Halos had a 3–1 lead over the Red Sox heading into the sixth inning. Manager Marcel Lachemann summoned Williams to replace starter Scott Sanderson with one on and one out. Williams walked his first two batters, then gave up an RBI single to Mike Greenwell. That was it for Mitch, and he was heavily booed on his way to the showers. (As a footnote, Mike Butcher replaced Williams and, after retiring the first batter, gave up a grand slam to Reggie Jefferson, sticking Williams with three earned runs.)

It didn't seem like things could get worse for Wild Thing, but somehow they did the very next night.

The Angels were already trailing Boston 4–1 when Williams came in to relieve Mike Bielecki. The first batter was Troy O'Leary, a lefty, so you had to figure Williams had a chance. Negative.

O'Leary ripped a two-run single to right to make it 7–1 Sox. Williams then walked John Valentin and faced another lefty, Mo Vaughn. Sure enough, Vaughn drove in three more with a towering homer, and just like that, it was 10–1.

As the ball sailed over the wall, Angels fans had seen enough.

It was Seat Cushion Night, and that didn't bode well for Mitch. As Vaughn crossed home plate, hundreds of fans turned their cushions into Frisbees, firing them at Williams. The game was actually delayed while the grounds crew cleaned up.

Now, I had seen some rowdy fans do some crazy things with giveaway items in the minor leagues, but this was a big-league stadium.

To his credit, Williams did manage to strike out Mike Macfarlane to end the inning, but obviously the damage was done. Mitch would only pitch six more times for the Angels—surprisingly not giving up any runs—before he was released.

Williams is now a mainstay on the MLB Network, and his often self-deprecating sense of humor has served him well. Even on that night, as his career was literally headed to the finish line, Mitch was able to put the seat cushion fiasco into proper perspective.

"Well, good thing it wasn't bow and arrow night," he joked.

Slump Buster

Baseball players have always been a superstitious lot. Some players have been known to wear the same underwear during a hitting streak. Heck, former Tiger Aubrey Huff will wear a thong when he's not hitting. Other guys avoid touching the baseline while running on and off the field.

Longtime reliever Turk Wendell had a whole list of quirks. Whenever an umpire gave him a new baseball, he insisted the ump roll it to him. If it was thrown, he'd let it go past him. If Turk began an inning, he would wave to the center fielder and wait for the gesture to be returned before proceeding. When his catcher stood up, Turk crouched down. Between innings, Wendell would always brush his teeth. And he would leap over the baseline when coming on or off the field.

Hall of Famer Wade Boggs was a study in superstition. He ate chicken every night for dinner and took exactly 100 ground balls during fielding drills. At 5:17, he took batting practice, and he ran at exactly 7:17. His eccentricities didn't stop there. During each of his at-bats, he drew the Hebrew word *chai*, meaning "life," in the batter's box. By the way, Boggs is not Jewish.

Some superstitions are certainly a little more "normal" than those of Wendell and Boggs. For years, when some players have been in a slump, they've tried to reverse their fortunes by wearing their socks high. And of course, there are the rally caps, too. But what happened in 1999 was something I had never experienced.

The Angels were in a funk. Grinding through a lost season, the Halos were 44–61 and struggling to score runs. They had lost 16 of their previous 18 games and were averaging less than three runs per game during that stretch.

What made this even more perplexing is that the lineup included an array of offensive talent such as All-Stars Garret Anderson, Troy Glaus, Jim Edmonds, Darin Erstad, and Mr. Angel himself, Tim Salmon. To make matters worse, the team's hitting coach that year was Hall of Famer Rod Carew, a seven-time batting champion.

Desperate times call for desperate measures. Carew tried anything and everything to solve the Angels' woes. He suggested that all nine batters use the same bat the first time through the order. For someone who was so particular about his bats to come up with this meant things were serious.

Manager Terry Collins overheard the plan being hatched in the dugout as the starters were trying to decided whose bat would be used. Collins quipped, "Make sure you pick one with some hits in it." It was decided that Jim Edmonds' bat would be used. After all, it was fresh since Edmonds had spent most of the season on the DL. Meanwhile, Gary DiSarcina's bat would be at the ready as a backup in case Edmonds' bat broke.

The game started, and while everyone on the Angels knew what was going on, nobody told home-plate umpire Tim Tschida. In the bottom of the first inning, Orlando Palmeiro led off the inning by taking a called third strike.

As Palmeiro took strike three, he dropped the bat at home plate for the next hitter, Gary DiSarcina, and walked back to the dugout. Tschida, not knowing what was happening, thought that Palmeiro was protesting by leaving his bat at the plate. One thing major league umpires won't put up with is being shown up. Tschida then ejected Palmeiro. So now the Halos had one out with one player already ejected. Palmeiro didn't know how to react or even how to explain the situation.

Terry Collins immediately ran from the dugout to explain what was happening. Once Tschida was clued in, he reversed his ejection call and Palmeiro was allowed to remain in the game.

In the broadcast booth, we had no idea what was going on. Nobody told us of the team's strategy, and we were truly confused.

After the next batter, DiSarcina, walked and dropped the bat right at home plate, we began to catch on in the booth. By the time the third hitter in the inning, Garret Anderson, strolled to the plate and picked up the bat, we finally put all of the pieces together. More importantly, so did the Angels offense.

One time through the lineup, the Angels went 4–8 with a walk and even picked up an RBI double from rookie Bengie Molina, his first major league hit. Molina recorded his first hit in the big leagues and it wasn't even his bat. Molina kept the bat for his collection.

The Angels would go on to put up 10 hits that night and beat the Royals 4–3. So you might be asking what happened to Jim Edmonds, the guy whose bat did all the damage.

He was 0–4. Go figure.

9/11

Certain events change the course of the world and in effect make us realize that, in the end, baseball is just a game.

There has been no event in U.S. history like September 11, 2001, the day our world changed forever.

I was broadcasting for the Angels at the time and remember my wife waking me up early as the news spread across the country. Being on west coast time, I was sound asleep when the first attack occurred. Of course, a few moments later, the second plane hit the second tower and the nightmare grew.

Like everyone else, I was glued to the television, watching the events unfold. And like everyone else, I was afraid to ask, "What's next?" I don't know how many hours we watched, but eventually the thought hit me—we had a game that night.

A few more hours went by, filled with priorities much bigger than baseball, before MLB announced that our game—and all games—were indeed canceled. A bit later, the Angels called me and asked if I would serve as the media pool reporter to disseminate the reaction of the players and coaching staff.

Of course, I agreed.

I rushed to the stadium and gathered a much sound as I could. Of all the interviews I'd done before or since, I'll never forget the range of emotions I heard that day.

Perhaps nobody was more fired up than reliever Troy Percival. The look in his eyes is something that was burned in my memory forever. He talked about the pride he had in his country and his anger toward those who had done this. In his eyes was pure fury. It was like he was ready to jump on a plane that moment and hunt down the perpetrators himself. I truly thought if he had been given the chance, he would have done just that.

MLB commissioner Bud Selig canceled the major league schedule through September 16 while the country tried to recover from the devastation. There was some question about whether teams should return at all to finish the season. We were all in unchartered territory.

When the schedule resumed, the Angels flew to Seattle. The games continued, but it was definitely not business as usual. I wouldn't be telling the truth if I said it was no big deal to get on a plane so soon after the attacks. We flew charter, but it was unnerving. Nobody knew what to expect.

On September 18, the Mariners beat the Angels 4–0 behind a three-hitter from Freddy Garcia to clinch at least a tie for the AL West title. (Seattle was dominant all season long, winning a record 116 games.) But it all seemed pointless. The season had continued, but the only thing that I truly remember from that night was the reaction of the sellout crowd.

Players from both teams lined the baselines as "God Bless America" and the national anthem were played, and several U.S. Marines presented the colors.

The following night, the Mariners clinched with a 5–0 win and celebrated with a spontaneous postgame parade around the infield with the Mariners players carrying the American flag.

I'm sure it was special for the Mariners to celebrate a historical season, but this was one time when even the opposition didn't mind seeing the other team celebrate.

CHAPTER 4
HEADING HOME

Landing the Dream Gig

Growing up in Detroit, I always wondered if I would get a chance to broadcast Tigers games in my career. In 2002, Josh Lewin left the Tigers to become the television voice of the Texas Rangers.

With the Tigers job now open, I decided to throw my hat in the ring and take a shot at the position. I had spent seven seasons in Anaheim with the Angels, but most of my experience was on the radio side. So I wasn't sure whether this would be enough to get me the job.

Television and radio are different beasts. In radio, the announcer is the eyes and ears for the listener. With TV, viewers can obviously see what is going on. Everything from the action to the weather to the color of the uniforms—it's all right there. In other words, less description is more. That is the biggest challenge for an announcer transitioning from radio to TV. Allowing the pictures to do the talking can take some getting used to.

The interview process was challenging. Fortunately, my Detroit background helped. I interviewed with FOX Sports Detroit's Executive Producer, John Tuohey (another Detroiter), and passed the first test.

Next up was a demo with analyst Kirk Gibson. Gibby was seven years removed from his 17-year big-league career, but he was just as intense.

We were shoved into a studio and had to call a couple innings of a random game replayed on a TV monitor. As fate would have it, the game we called featured Tigers pitcher Steve Sparks, who had spent a couple of seasons with the Angels, so I was familiar with him. This gave me a little peace of mind. The demo went well, and I waited to see if it was good enough to land the job.

After a small round of negotiations, I was offered the job and accepted.

Getting any TV job was a huge deal for me. To do it in my hometown carried some additional pressure. Now I wasn't just working for myself—I was representing my family.

Josh Lewin is a very talented broadcaster. He left big footsteps for me to try to fill. Of course, there were the unapproachable legacies of Ernie Harwell and George Kell. This was the big leagues, literally.

Whenever there is a change, it takes people a while to adjust and accept.

I think it took several years for Tigers fans to become familiar with me and vice versa.

Now, twelve years later, I've learned that it's not about living up to anyone else's expectations or reputations. Nobody expects more from me than me. I've tried to tell the story of the ballgame while providing context and reacting as a fan.

Every baseball game has its own script, whether it's Magglio Ordonez putting the Tigers into the World Series with a home run or Armando Galarraga throwing the (im)perfect game. You never know what is going to happen, and after all this time, I finally feel like I belong—which is kind of a strange statement from someone who was born here.

A Dream Come True

Every kid grows up, hoping to be a major league player. And for 99.99 percent of them, that never happens. I was no different. Fortunately, I came to that realization pretty early, and my attention turned to broadcasting.

It's ironic that one of the biggest names in the history of Tigers baseball—in the history of the game, for that matter—was someone who never played a single inning. He was the voice of the Tigers, the man who made listeners feel like they were at the game from the comfort of their own home.

Ernie Harwell spoke to us from the corner of Michigan and Trumbull, and night after night he told me about a game that I couldn't wait to explore. Whether it was a "foul ball caught by a man from Clarkston," or someone who was "caught standing there like a house on the side of the road," every game was an adventure.

Working my way through high school and college, I started to take the necessary steps to make my hopes come true. My dream was to become the voice of the Tigers, but my secret desire was to work just one inning with Harwell, one of the game's great voices.

On June 1, 2003, fantasy became reality, and it was even better than I ever could have hoped.

I had the privilege of meeting Ernie eight years earlier when I was a young broadcaster working for the California Angels. The Tigers were in town, and I finally summoned up the courage to meet my idol.

I was nervous for obvious reasons. How often do you meet someone you really admire? And what if he/she fails to live up to your expectations?

Think about it—as a kid sometimes you wait in line for an autograph from your favorite player, and he stiffs you. Meeting your idol is risky business.

Unless your idol is Ernie Harwell. He spent more time with me than I had any right to expect. We talked about how my job was going, where I grew up, and how proud my parents were. Then Ernie did something without being asked, something I've appreciated since the day I met him.

During his game broadcast, he casually dropped in a greeting. "Mr. and Mrs. Impemba, I met your son, Mario, today, and I want to tell you he's doing great!"

While I was across the country, working with the Angels, Ernie dropped a personal greeting to my parents on the air.

———

On a beautiful June day in 2003, the Tigers were playing the Yankees, and my broadcast partner was unavailable. You really couldn't come up with a better pinch hitter for the broadcast than Ernie. Ernie had retired following the 2002 season and was available to fill in.

I remember getting a call from our executive producer, John Tuohey.

"We've found someone to fill in as the analyst," Tuohey said.

"Great. Who?" I asked.

"Ernie said he would be happy to do it."

"Ernie? As in Harwell?"

"Yep, it should be fun."

I remember feeling excited and nervous at the same time. I was going to get a chance to work with a personal idol. I thought to myself, *Don't screw this up.*

As if the day wasn't special enough, it just so happened that there was a sense of history in the air. Roger Clemens was going for his 300th career win.

Veteran Tigers broadcaster Ernie Harwell pauses during a break in the action in the fifth inning of the Tigers game against the New York Yankees on Sunday, October 3, 1993, at Yankee Stadium in New York *(AP Photo/Paul Hurschmann)*

It didn't figure to be much of a struggle—the Tigers were on their way to 119 losses. Of course I wanted to give the event its proper due, but I'll be honest. I wouldn't have cared if this was a little league game. I was living my all-time dream scenario!

My game plan that day was really to just stay out of the way and set up Ernie as much as possible. But Harwell had other ideas. He wanted the game to be the story, not his appearance.

The Tigers trailed 7–1 but mustered a comeback with five runs in the fifth inning, tying it up in the seventh. Then the two teams played...and played... and played.

My dream game with Ernie nearly turned into two dream games—the score was tied going into the 17th inning! Alfonso Soriano and Jorge Posada both deposited Steve Sparks' knuckleballs into the seats, and New York ended up winning 10–9. Not only did I get to work with Ernie, but we did 17 innings of baseball that day.

A photo that we took in the booth that day and a tape of the game telecast are two of my most prized possessions. Yes, the Tigers lost the game, and I would go on to work with Ernie several times over the next few years, but that day, my first game with the great Ernie Harwell, is something I will never forget.

———

My feelings for Ernie made September 17, 2009, all the more difficult. A few weeks earlier, Ernie had been diagnosed with terminal bile-duct cancer, and he knew that he didn't have much time left to live.

Again, showing his incredible graciousness, he wanted a chance to say thank you and goodbye to Tigers fans. Of course, it was the fans who really owed the debt of gratitude.

Between innings of an otherwise meaningless game against the Kansas City Royals, Ernie stepped to home plate and gave one of the most memorable, eloquent speeches I've ever heard. He had no notes—this came straight from the heart.

The emotion at Comerica Park was tangible. It seemed trivial to go on with the game from that point. But that's what Ernie wanted. I still get chills thinking about it today.

That next January, I was home watching a college basketball game when my cell phone rang. We had just finished our Tigers Caravan tour through the state, and I was exhausted. I didn't recognize the number, so I let it go to voicemail. About five minutes later, during a commercial in the game, I decided to take a listen.

The word *horrified* perfectly sums up my emotions. Ernie, his health now failing at a more rapid rate, had called me, and I didn't answer.

"Just great!" I yelled at no one in particular.

"Who was it?" my wife, Cathy, asked.

"It was only Ernie Harwell," I said. "But that's okay. Watching this basketball game was more important than taking his call anyway," I said sarcastically.

I called him back immediately and, of course, Ernie was unflappable. Facing his imminent death, he wanted to thank me for our friendship and essentially say goodbye to me. That was the last time I spoke to my idol.

I still have his number in my cell phone contacts to this day. I can't bear to delete it.

Running from History

Any broadcaster can take a winning team and make it sound great. He can even take a decent team and make it sound good. In 2003, I had the challenge of making one of the worst teams in baseball history sound… well, not as bad.

The 2003 Tigers were overmatched. This was before the acquisitions of Ivan "Pudge" Rodriguez, Magglio Ordonez, and Carlos Guillen. These were the days of Warren Morris, Alex Sanchez, and Kevin Witt. Before the Tigers embarked on a golden era of their history, they nearly made a different type of history—the wrong kind.

Tigers legend Alan Trammell was brought in to manage a young and inexperienced club. "Tram" was a lifelong Tiger, spending all 20 of his big-league seasons wearing the Old English D. He had seen the best of times and the worst of times in his borderline Hall of Fame career. He was the World Series MVP in 1984 and also struggled through seasons in last place. The Tigers perhaps hoped he could bring some of his magic to a team in desperate need of it.

The season began with nine straight losses, and the Tigers were outscored 54–14. It was pretty obvious that this was going to be a long season.

When Nate Cornejo beat the White Sox on April 12, the Tigers finally had one in the win column. We all hoped there was no place to go but up, but we were wrong. The team lost their next eight in a row, falling to 1–17.

Watching a team play so poorly was difficult for anyone. But for a lifelong Tigers fan like myself, it was so uncomfortable watching Trammel, one of my favorite players, having to endure a season like this.

The Tigers limped into the All-Star break with a 25–67 record. Let's put this in simple mathematical terms. To reach 25–67, the team actually had to *improve* on their start to go 24–50 for the rest of the first half.

After getting a few days to relax during the break—Dimitri Young was the lone All-Star—the Tigers came out of the blocks, staggering to a 6–30 record. The chase with history was on.

For more than 40 years, the 1962 Mets were the standard for modern-day futility. But at least that mish-mosh of minimal talent was an expansion team. The Tigers were giving the Mets a run for their money, but it wouldn't be decided until the season's last week.

The Tigers would wake up on September 23 with a record of 38–118. They had lost 16 of their last 17 games. To avoid history, they would have to do the unthinkable—win five of their last six games, something they hadn't come close to accomplishing all year long.

In the first game, Mike Maroth avoided becoming a 22-game loser as A.J. Hinch, Warren Morris, and Craig Monroe all went deep in a 15–6 rout over Kansas City. I was glad for Maroth, one of the most decent guys I've met in baseball. Even as he was facing the infamy of becoming the first pitcher in 23 years to lose 20 games, Mike took the ball without complaint, even after his grandmother passed away. He never deserved what he got that season, but I don't know anyone who would have dealt with it better.

The next day, the Tigers erupted (okay, they actually scored two runs on singles, one on a walk, and one on a sacrifice fly) for four runs in the first inning, and Shane Loux held on for his first major league win.

Minnesota came to town for a four-game series to close out the year. Thanks to their recent hot streak, the Tigers needed to take three of the four games to avoid infamy.

The first game was a stunner, as Nate Robertson out-dueled future Cy Young winner Johan Santana, and Shane Halter belted an eleventh-inning home run as the Tigers won 5–4.

The tables turned on Friday night, as Michael Cuddyer's eleventh-inning blast gave the Twins a 5–4 win.

It was down to two games. Two wins, and the Tigers would avoid history. One win or no wins, and they'd live forever—for the wrong reasons.

The day didn't get off to a good start. The Twins erupted for four runs in the fourth and three more in the fifth. Brade Radke, a 14-game winner, was cruising on the mound. But manager Ron Gardenhire pulled Radke after just

80 pitches through five innings. The Twins were in first place and would throw Radke in Game 2 of the playoffs against the Yankees.

In the bottom of the seventh, Craig Monroe smashed an RBI double, and Carlos Pena drove in two more. Now it was 8–4. Then in the eighth, a bases-loaded walk to Young plus two more huge hits from Monroe and Pena tied the game at 8–8. The Tigers couldn't possibly…. Or could they?

You better believe they could. With Sanchez on third, 46-year-old Jesse Orosco, in his last major league season, threw a wild pitch, and the Tigers pulled out an impossible 9–8 win.

That set up the drama. One game, baseball's most infamous record on the line. This was as close as we were getting to a playoff game in 2003.

As fate would have it, Mike Maroth was back on the hill. Mike had avoided the loss in his last start but was still 8–21 on the season. The odds were not good that the Tigers would win—Maroth had lost consecutive starts on all but two occasions all year.

Yet the Tigers bats continued to mash, putting up seven runs in the sixth inning and holding for a 9–4 victory. It may not seem like a great accomplishment, finishing with the second-worst record in baseball history, but it's a heck of a lot better being No. 2.

On the postgame show, I had a videotape of the 1962 Mets season in my hand. As we ended the segment, I tossed the tape over my shoulder and said, "The '62 Mets will not have company. The record is still all theirs."

Big Market Transformation

Detroit's population has taken a hit over the years. In 2003, its population was just a hair less than 927,000. Five years later, it was about 912,600. But somehow, in baseball terms, Detroit had transformed from a medium-small market into a big one. That change made an enormous difference in the standings and expectations for the Tigers.

While in many ways, today's team is a who's who of baseball thanks to names like Justin Verlander, Miguel Cabrera, and Torii Hunter, the 2003 roster was more of a "Who's that?"

Not very many recognizable names dotted the roster. Do you remember names like Alex Sanchez, Warren Morris, and Gene Kingsale? They were all nice guys, but they were borderline major leaguers at best. While today's starting pitching rotation is considered among the league's best, that team featured Gary Knotts, Nate Cornejo, and Adam Bernero. No wonder the Tigers had to win five of their last six games to avoid the 1962 Mets as the only team to lose 120 games.

It seemed that once his team hit rock bottom, owner Mike Ilitch changed his philosophy. Ilitch is and has always been a baseball guy first. However, while the Tigers languished, the Red Wings had won three Stanley Cup championships. The first major step in rebuilding the Tigers was signing Ivan "Pudge" Rodriguez, followed by Magglio Ordonez. Their signings brought credibility, and three years later, Detroit was miraculously in the 2006 World Series. That definitely whetted the fans' appetites for a title, and the 2012 and 2013 teams featured three players (Cabrera, Verlander, and Fielder) earning at least $20 million.

When casual fans look at big-market teams such as the Yankees or Red Sox, the assumption is that those teams can just buy the best players. That's not entirely true. Sure, they can attract higher-salaried players with their additional funds. They can also buy their way out of mistakes, if needed. But to sustain excellence, smart teams use the extra money to develop their farm systems. Under the guidance of team president and general manager David Dombrowski, the Tigers are a great example of this strategy. Dave has mastered the dance between free agency, trades, and drafts. Sometimes, even when a player doesn't work out, the Tigers have been able to use him as a bargaining chip.

The 2004 MLB Amateur Draft was a great example of what you can do by spending a few bucks. San Diego had the first pick, and being in a perennial small-market team, the Padres went for the affordable pick and chose high schooler Matt Bush. Of course they knew that he was a reach, but again, he wouldn't break the bank. The Tigers, coming off that awful 2003 season, went for talent and drafted a right-handed college pitcher named Justin Verlander. I think you know how that worked out.

Because of the team's willingness to spend money on difficult-to-sign players, the Tigers have ended up with some premium talent. For example, in the 2006 draft, Detroit took a shot at pitcher Andrew Miller, a player the experts said would stay at the University of North Carolina.

Dombrowski took a shot at the 6'10" lefty, and he was playing in the majors within a couple of months. Both Miller and outfielder Cameron Maybin were considered two of the best prospects in all of baseball, untouchable in any deal...until the Tigers traded both of them to Florida for Dontrelle Willis and a guy named Miguel Cabrera. That trade showed how the team's ability to spend money on scouting brought them two assets, Miller and Maybin, who could be turned into Willis and Cabrera.

But I also mentioned that deep pockets can give teams the ability to erase mistakes. The Tigers gave Willis a contract extension before he ever pitched for Detroit. The D-Train was never on track with the Tigers. The lefty was paid $29 million for two wins in the Old English D. If this happened to the Tampa Bay Rays, for example, it would have been devastating, and they might not have been to afford Cabrera's extension. But through ownership's commitment, Willis' dismal tenure left only collateral damage.

Along with higher payroll, of course, comes higher expectations. When your payroll is among MLB's top five, fans want more. I can't speak for everyone, but it's a heckuva lot more fun broadcasting for a team that has a legitimate chance to win.

Money alone does not necessarily guarantee results. The Tigers have spent wisely in the past, giving Anibal Sanchez five years for more than $80 million and Joaquin Benoit three years and $16.5 million to initially set up at the back end of the pen. Both players have proven to be worth every penny.

The Tigers' payroll is as competitive as most in baseball. That's a far cry from the days when the team payroll was a little more than a third of what it is today.

Center Field

Growing up in Detroit during the 1970s and early 1980s, my dream was simple, concise, and (I thought) reachable—to play center field for the Tigers. By my teen years, I made peace with the grim reality that it wasn't going to happen.

But I was always riveted by the position. Guys who played center field were always great athletes—Fred Lynn in Boston, Andre Dawson up in Montreal, and Ken Griffey in Seattle. But my guy was Chet Lemon at Tiger Stadium. "The Jet" didn't really run to balls—he glided. Yes, Lemon was a good hitter, but it was his graceful play in center that mesmerized me.

I'm not sure if it's because of those childhood memories, but I've always loved watching great center-field play. Center and shortstop are really the two glamour positions in the field. During my career, I've been fortunate to cover three of the best center fielders in the game.

In Anaheim, Jim Edmonds was really more of a ballerina with a football player's mentality. When he set his tracks on the ball, it was going to get caught. And if he had to run into a wall to do it…well, good luck to the wall.

Edmonds retired with eight Gold Gloves, and this wasn't a case of winning based on reputation. Toward the end of his career, Edmonds played some first base, which was really a sad sight for those of us who marveled at his playing ability.

There is no question about what was the best display of that ability. It was June 1997, and Edmonds' Angels were playing Kansas City. The matchup was really nothing special. But once again, you never know what you're going to see.

Royals infielder David Howard hit a shot to dead center. This was surely going to the wall for at least a double, if not more. Edmonds was playing shallow—a reasonable move given Howard's career total of 11 home runs.

Immediately, Jim turned and retreated toward the wall. Without even turning, he leaped—a full-out dive at the warning track. The ball went over his head, but Edmonds made the grab.

In the booth, partner Bob Starr and I sat in stunned silence. There were no words to do the play justice. Not only was this the greatest catch I had ever seen, it may very well be the best catch of all-time. If this happened in the postseason, especially with today's technology and camera angles, it would probably be one of the most replayed catches in baseball history.

———

Since coming back to Detroit, I've had the privilege of covering two guys who have carried on the Chet Lemon tradition—Curtis Granderson and Austin Jackson.

In May 2009, Justin Verlander was locked in a duel with Cliff Lee. JV really had it going on, allowing just two hits during the first eight innings. The Tigers led 1–0 going into the bottom of the ninth. After a leadoff walk, Verlander got the next out. Up came All-Star Grady Sizemore. In a moment, it seemed to be over.

Sizemore ripped a shot to dead center, and it looked like a game-winning home run. But then, out of nowhere, Granderson not only tracked it down but then leaped over the center-field wall to save the game! Given the situation, it was one of the most dramatic catches I had ever seen. One of my friends was recovering from back surgery and watching the game in the hospital. His response pretty much said it all. He told me later, "I had to check to see if it was all a dream."

Before the 2011 season, Granderson was dealt in a three-way deal with the Yankees and Diamondbacks. Grandy ended up in pinstripes, and the Tigers picked up (among others) New York's top prospect, center fielder Austin Jackson.

A-Jax has plenty of potential with the bat, but from day one, he's been a Gold Glove–caliber defender. If there was any doubt, he proved it in June 2010 with one of the most dramatic catches I've ever seen.

It was known as the "Imperfect Game" against Cleveland, and pitcher Armando Galarraga received more notoriety than any pitcher who threw an actual perfect game.

The first image people remember, of course, is Jim Joyce blowing an out call at first base for what should have been the final out of the ballgame. But just before that, Jackson made a catch that was really beyond description.

Galarraga was sailing along beautifully through eight innings, never really having any hard-hit balls. But to lead off the ninth was veteran Mark Grudzielanek—a former All-Star, and a tough guy to get out. Grudzielanek hit the ball on a rope to left-center, and I knew this would be at least a double. Jackson was fast, but there was no way he'd be able to track this down… was there?

Like he was shot out of a cannon, A-Jax sprinted in and made the perfect game-saving catch. Jackson will hopefully have a long, productive career, but I will guarantee he will never make another pressure-filled catch like that one.

As if to pour (more) salt in the Indians' wound, Austin killed the Tribe again in 2011.

It was late August, and the Tigers had finally caught the front-running Indians and were now trying to put some distance between them. Things looked good as Detroit jumped out to a 7–0 lead. But Cleveland wouldn't give up and actually cut the lead to 8–6 on a Travis Hafner RBI in the sixth.

The Tigers led 8–7 in the ninth when Jose Valverde came in for the save. Papa Grande put the first two men on base via walk and hit by pitch. With one out, the Tribe had men on second and third with pinch hitter Matt LaPorta at the plate.

He hit a shot to center that, of course, Jackson snagged with a running catch. Kosuke Fukudome tried to score, but Action Jackson nailed him at the plate with a perfect throw.

A-Jax had singlehandedly done it to Cleveland again. The Tigers' AL Central lead was 4½ games, and they never looked back.

Why Tigers Fans are the Best

When I make the statement that Tigers fans are the best in all of baseball, it might sound like I'm biased, and of course, I am. Being a native Michigander, and spending most of my career here, what else would you expect?

But I do truly believe that I am the luckiest broadcaster in the major leagues because not only do I cover my hometown team, but I do it with the best fans around.

Why are they the best? There are several reasons.

The first factor is how every fan buys in. How many times each day do you see the Old English D? It's on shirts, jackets, and naturally, caps. I don't think you see anything like that anywhere else in the country. In New York, for example, you see the NY logo, but some people are rooting for the Yankees, while others are rooting for the Mets. In Chicago, the loyalty is split between the Cubs and White Sox. California has the Dodgers and Angels. The closest thing to what we have here might be in Boston, where you do see a lot of stuff with the big B on it.

In each market, of course, the fans want the home team to win. In some places more than others, they expect them to. But I get the feeling here in Detroit that the fans truly support the Tigers like nowhere else.

If the team struggles, yes, the fans will voice their dissatisfaction. But if it's possible to differentiate boos, Detroit fans lack the venom of some other major markets. (This may not be true for the Lions, but for the Tigers, I say it is.) It feels like fans are booing the action, not the player. For example, if Justin Verlander were to give up five home runs in a start, then naturally fans would be upset, and they might boo. But given what JV has done for the franchise, he'd almost get a pass that night.

A contrast occurred a few years ago in Boston. Designated hitter David Ortiz was in the worst slump of his career, and Red Sox fans booed him every time he made an out, actually calling for his release. This is a guy who led them to two World Series titles, and that's how they treat him?

The same thing happened in New York where Derek Jeter struggled through the worst slump of his Hall of Fame career in 2010. He had just won his fifth World Series in pinstripes the year before, but when his average fell to .270, he was a bum. Boos cascaded down on Jeter as fans actually suggested New York should let him go to another team to finish his career. Even the Yankees decided to play hardball during negotiations and told Jeter to explore the market and find a better deal.

Fortunately for the team and their fans, Derek made it clear that he only wanted to play for the Yankees, and while he wasn't happy with the contract, he did sign it and went on to regain his All-Star form and collect career hit No. 3,000.

Compare those two examples to Detroit. When Miguel Cabrera had not one but two off-field issues, fans never booed him. When he returned to the team on each of the following Opening Days, he got the loudest ovation of any player. And keep in mind, Miguel was not a guy who came up through the

Tigers system; he was acquired in a trade, so he hadn't built up as much equity as someone like Verlander.

Gary Sheffield was someone who appreciated the Detroit fans. Sheff had experienced just about everything during his career, playing in laid-back markets like Florida and Los Angeles, as well as the fishbowl of New York.

By the time he came to Detroit in 2007, he was on the back nine of a potential Hall of Fame career. His two years here didn't go particularly well—he hit .247 with just 44 home runs. But I remember a conversation with him talking about how mild (for lack of a better word) the fans and media were in Detroit, and he just smiled because he knew how well he had it.

———

It was painful to watch Jose Valverde struggle in 2012. The prior year he was nearly perfect in racking up a team-record 49 saves. He was a free agent investment that really paid off.

Now like his predecessor, Todd Jones, Papa Grande tended to make things exciting. The 1-2-3 innings were not the rule, especially in non-save situations. But the bottom line was that more times than not, he was smiling and dancing at the end.

But 2012 was clearly a different year. Papa struggled. His fastball declined, and so did his strikeouts. Fans were frustrated all year, pleading for a better alternative. In the last month of the season, Valverde seemingly lost his No. 1 asset—his confidence.

In the playoffs, he bottomed out. First, he blew a save in Oakland with a chance to clinch the series. After the Tigers escaped the A's, Valverde gave up a dramatic ninth-inning home run to Raul Ibanez in Game One of the ALCS. The Tigers won that series, but it was the last time we would see Papa Grande in a critical situation as a Tiger that year.

But even as upset as Tigers fans were at Valverde, they were willing to see if he had anything left when the Tigers re-signed him the following year.

———

The kindness of the fans here extends beyond the players, as well. I can't tell you how many letters, cards, or just nice greetings I've received from fans on a daily basis.

Twitter has opened up a whole new avenue for fans to interact with players and teams. Some fans just don't like you and will constantly let you know, but for the most part, the support has been overwhelming.

Even the most successful season can be such a grind. Time away from our families, going from one city to another, sometimes waking up and not knowing which state we're in—it all takes a toll. But the hospitality and support we receive makes it all worthwhile.

One of the times I feel it the most is during the postseason. As you may know, FOX Sports Detroit does not have the broadcast rights to carry playoff games. That typically falls to either TBS, the MLB Network, or FOX Network. It's a really frustrating situation for us. We spend all season with these guys, more time with the players than with our own families, and just as things really get good, we have to watch like fans.

So when the Tigers are home for those playoff games, I will usually work from the park on our postgame show. If I stopped for every person who shouted encouragement to us on the way to our seats, I'd never see a pitch. It makes you realize how special the fans are here.

People are always saying how much more they enjoy the job Rod Allen and I do versus the national broadcasters, which is so kind, but it's also a bit unfair. Being with the team all year, we know all of the story lines. If you're Joe Buck or Ernie Johnson, it's tough to try and follow every team and sound like an expert on each one. The national broadcasters do a great job with major challenges.

The other place where I feel overwhelming support is during our winter Tigers Caravan. We travel in small groups, typically three or four players in addition to guys like myself, Rod, or Dan Dickerson, and we get to meet fans all over the state to talk Tigers baseball. It's amazing how ravenous fans are, whether we're coming off a good year or not. I think baseball is the one sport that people like to talk about more than any other, no matter what team they cheer for. It's on visits like this where we really get a sense of how much we've become part of fans' lives.

Number Six

One of the most exciting parts about covering Spring Training is walking into the clubhouse and seeing a certain someone at his locker.

No. 6 may be pushing 80 years in age, but it's 80 years young, not old. No, he's not getting ready to play—it's been 30 years since Al Kaline last graced the Old English D as an active player, but "Mr. Tiger" still shows off the enthusiasm he had when he made his big-league debut as an 18-year-old in 1953.

In just his second full season in the majors, Kaline became the youngest batting champion in baseball history, hitting .340 at the tender age of 20. He played a total 22 years, making 15 All-Star teams and winning 10 Gold Gloves. He was easily voted into the Hall of Fame on his first attempt, with more than 88 percent of baseball writers checking his box on the ballot, which at the time was the 12th best percentage of all time.

Al still has an important role with the team as a special advisor to president and GM David Dombrowski. I think the Tigers have been very smart to put Kaline's vast baseball knowledge to use. One thing that makes this Hall of Famer different than many of his counterparts is that he not only still loves the game, but he's also willing to share that passion not only with players but with fans, too.

One of my spring training highlights came in March 2013 in the clubhouse at Joker Marchant Stadium in Lakeland, Florida.

One of the big stories on this star-filled team was super-prospect Nick Castellanos. The just-turned 21-year-old broke into baseball as a third baseman. With MVP Miguel Cabrera providing a Triple Crown–sized roadblock, the Tigers' brass decided to move Castellanos to the outfield in the middle of the 2012 campaign. So who did Dombroski want teaching his best prospect the nuances of a new position? Arguably the best defensive right fielder of all time, Al Kaline. Who else?

One of the things Castellanos would have to master as he made the transition to the outfield is the ability to compartmentalize different parts of the game. Kaline believes that most young players take bad at-bats into the field with them. One reason Al was such a great player was that he could separate offense and defense. It happens all the time. A hotshot prospect never

Hall of Fame outfielder Al Kaline, watches batting practice before an exhibition spring training game against the Toronto Blue Jays on Friday, March 15, 2013 in Lakeland, Florida. *(AP Photo/Carlos Osorio)*

reaches his potential because he's lacking mental toughness. Kaline had it by the truckload.

We've all seen the little leaguer picking dandelions in the outfield, waiting for a ball to come his way. It can be exactly the same in the big leagues, minus the dandelions.

"You have to push yourself," Kaline said. "You can get bored in the outfield, and you have to tell yourself that the next ball is coming to [you]. It's not easy because you can take your at-bats out to the field with you. The really tough individuals separate a bad at-bat and their responsibilities on defense."

That mental toughness and focus is also necessary if a player has any thoughts of being a quality major league hitter.

"I used to drive to the games at Tiger Stadium with Bill Freehan, and he would tell me that I wasn't a good driving partner because I never said a word the entire ride," Kaline said. "Truth was, I was thinking about that night's pitcher and how he pitched me the last time I faced him. We'd arrive at the stadium and I wouldn't remember anything about the drive. It's a miracle I didn't get us killed."

Kaline had a reputation as being stoic at the ballpark. It was a reputation born from focus.

"I was always criticized because I never smiled on the field," he said. "My wife always used to ask me why I would never wave to her in the stands. That's how focused I was."

Kaline's focus and mental toughness was also the result of a fear of embarrassing himself on the field. So was his decision to retire when he did, instead of prolonging his career and collecting a paycheck.

He finished his career with 399 home runs. Instead of coming back for one more year to reach 400, Kaline called it quits.

"I could see that I had lost my skills, and I didn't want to hang around and embarrass myself," he said. "I never wanted to take a paycheck if I felt I didn't earn it."

It's a refreshing attitude that isn't always prevalent in today's game. Yes, Al Kaline is approaching the big 8–0, but the current generation of today's players could learn a lot from spending a few minutes with No. 6. If Nick Castellanos becomes a huge star, I'm guessing he'll remember the lessons he learned from his Hall of Fame tutor.

The Bird Is the Word

There are once-in-a-generation talents—players who combine tremendous skill with infectious charisma to grab a city's attention. And they don't let go.

The Detroit Tigers of the mid 1970s definitely needed a boost. The World Series championship of 1968 was in the rearview mirror. The year 1972 provided a highlight for the team, led by the charismatic Billy Martin, with an American League East title. The Tigers lost in the ALCS to Oakland that season. But as was usually the case with Billy, the magic didn't have a long shelf life.

A tough-nosed manager who wasn't afraid of anyone, Martin would last barely one more year and was fired in September 1973. The Tigers lost 102

Pitcher Mark Fidrych, is shown sitting in the Tigers dugout before a game on August 10, 1976, in Detroit, Michigan. He was the American League rookie of the year in 1976 when he went 19–9 with a 2.34 ERA. He spent all five of his major league seasons with the Detroit Tigers, compiling a 29–19 record and a 3.10 ERA. *(AP Photo)*

games just two years later, and a pair of last-place finishes in 1974 and 1975 left the club looking for a spark.

Little did anyone in Detroit know that a spark was right around the corner, in the form of a gangly, shaggy-haired Massachusetts boy who was drafted in the tenth round.

Mark "The Bird" Fidrych burst on the scene in 1976 as an unheralded 21-year-old. With a seemingly rubber arm and an array of zany antics, the Bird came out of nowhere to create a stir the likes of which Detroit had never seen. He manicured the mound. He talked to the baseball. Oh, and he won 19 games and started in the All-Star Game.

Every time Fidrych took the hill, old Tiger Stadium was packed. That the team had a losing record, finishing in fifth place, didn't matter. The Bird was a phenomenon. Tigers fans still talk about his complete-game victory over the American League Champion New York Yankees on *Monday Night Baseball* in late June.

Bird was a shooting star in every sense of the word. Almost as quickly as he took over Motown, he was finished as a big leaguer.

The injuries started innocently enough. First, Fidrych tore cartilage in his knee in the outfield during spring training in 1977. When he returned, he was as good as ever. He lost his first two starts, but then ripped off six straight complete-game victories.

But on an early July night in Baltimore, Fidrych felt his arm go "dead." It wasn't until several years later that doctors diagnosed him with a torn rotator cuff—a death penalty for pitchers back then. Bird would only win four more games in his career.

Fidrych spent another five years battling in the minors, trying to somehow regain his past glory. He never accomplish that, but it wasn't for lack of trying. His manager in AAA Evansville was a guy you've probably heard of— Jim Leyland.

Fast-forward to April 2013 when the Tigers visited Anaheim for a series with the Angels. The emergence of Mike Trout had sparked a conversation in the manager's office. One of the writers asked Leyland if he had ever seen a rookie season as dominant as Mike Trout's historic 2012 campaign.

"I've never seen anyone break in that was more talented than Trout, but for a player that just captured the baseball world, Mark Fidrych would be No. 1 on my list," Leyland said. "I've never seen a guy [who] impacted the game like he did, and he only played once every five days. I've never seen anything like the hype that surrounded his starts."

Eventually, Fidrych stopped chasing the dream in 1983 when his career ended with the AAA team for his hometown Red Sox. After his playing days were over, Fidrych settled in Northborough, a Boston suburb, and lived on his farm. He would occasionally visit the booth when we played at Fenway Park.

On our visit to Boston in 2004, our producer, Mark Iacofano, told me that the Bird was coming to the ball park that night and wanted to know if I would like him to join us in the booth for a couple of innings.

"Sure, the fans in Detroit would love to reconnect with the Bird," I said.

Normally I'm not crazy about guests in the booth for more than half an inning. I want to be able to do our job and focus on the game without any distractions. This was definitely an exception to the rule, and Bird knew it. He joined us in the second inning, and a couple of innings turned into the rest of the game. That broadcast is one I will never forget.

The Bird told stories of his playing days and the phenomena of his rise to the big leagues. I don't remember if it was a long- or short-running game. I only remember that I wished it had gone on a little longer. With Fidrych, there was no hidden agenda. He was all about straight-forward language and a tell-it-like-it-is outlook on life.

Mark was a throwback to old-school baseball. We talked about how many of today's pitchers think their job is to throw six innings or 100 pitches, then leave it up to the bullpen. The Bird was not programmed that way. In his day, pitchers expected to complete what they started. In that magical year of 1976, the rookie led the American League with 24 complete games—despite not entering the rotation until May. Fidrych would end up throwing 34 complete in just 56 major league starts. Think about that.

It really was great having Fidrych in the booth, but there was one nerve-racking part. I think I had my finger on the mute button for three straight hours, because with Bird up there, you never knew what he would say next, or if it would include any expletives. Whatever he did say, it was in his thick New England accent. Nobody would ever wonder where he grew up.

Even after he retired, he was always the Bird, but it was in a good way, not like a big-timer. He treated everyone like a friend—like he knew you for years.

I couldn't help but think how lucky I was to be sitting next to a guy that, in his own way, had impacted the city of Detroit and all of baseball in a way not seen before or since. The effect Bird had was immeasurable. It gave Tigers fans, including yours truly, something to be proud of.

Unfortunately, Mark Fidrych died in April 2009 due to an accident while working on his truck.

There surely won't be another one like him.

Detroit's Holiday

There's nothing like Opening Day, and I've never experienced any Opening Day to rival Detroit's. There's always a sense of renewal and hope, no matter what the realistic expectations are for that year's Tigers. It's about breaking out the new cap, tasting the season's first hot dog, and keeping score after a long winter's break.

It's practically a state holiday. Dads take their kids out of school. Fans pour into downtown Detroit early and stay late. Since Comerica Park opened in 2000, the Tigers have routinely drawn anywhere from 40,000 to 45,000 fans on Opening Day. Even in the 119-loss campaign of 2003, 40,427 diehard Tigers fans braved the cold (and some bad baseball) to cheer on their team. In 2013, the Tigers Opening Day crowd established a Comerica Park record at 45,051.

Here are my top Comerica Park memories (in no particular order) on Opening Day:

2013: Expectations for the 2013 Tigers were World Series or bust. After getting swept in the Fall Classic, Detroit added Torii Hunter and welcomed Victor Martinez to an already potent lineup.

Still, the season started with a rough patch—two losses in Minnesota to a bad Twins team. The already-suspect bullpen was causing worry throughout

Detroit, and some cynical fans were flashing back to the highly touted 2008 team, which was considered the AL favorite but finished in last place.

That team, however, didn't have Prince Fielder. In the home opener against the depleted Yankees, the big man put himself right in the record books. First came a close call. Fielder hit a shot to right that former Tiger Brennan Boesch caught diving against the wall. In Fielder's next two at-bats, though, the only people who were able to make the catch were the fans.

The first home run came when Prince chased a pitch near his eyes. That one was "only" a few rows into the right-field stands. There was no doubting the second one. Fielder put all his weight into it and crushed another homer. In all, Fielder drove in five runs and the Tigers routed the Yanks 8–3. Prince put it best: "It was a dream come true. I've got my boys with me, and my family is here."

On the mound, Doug Fister didn't have his best stuff, but he gutted through five decent innings. Then second-year man Drew Smyly, who was edged out for a spot in the starting rotation, pitched four perfect innings.

2009: After the previous year's disaster, getting off to a good start was paramount for the 2009 team. Before the game, there was a dramatic, booming, military flyover. After the first pitch, it was the Tigers' bats that did the booming. Miguel Cabrera ended the drama early, with a huge grand slam against Texas starter Kris Benson. Officially, 44,588 fans went home happy as the Tigers scored early and often in a 14–2 blowout.

2005: The Tigers of the early 2000s didn't have much to celebrate. Maybe we should have known that Opening Day 2005 was going to be special when the temperature hit a remarkable 70 degrees.

You know how I mentioned that sense of renewal every April? On this day, it was Dmitri Young's turn to shine. In what manager Alan Trammell called "the greatest performance I've ever seen on Opening Day," the "Meat Hook" went deep not once, not twice, but three times.

Dmitri had a good yet checkered career, but he was all smiles on this day. Young became just the third player in big-league history to hit three homers on Opening Day. He finished 4–4 with five RBI in an 11–2 win over Kansas City.

2004: One year after the Tigers set an American League record with 119 losses, fans were expecting more of the same in 2004. The final record will show the Tigers finished with a 72–90 record, but at least they started well.

First came a stunning three-game sweep in Toronto. (For a little perspective, the 2003 Tigers had a total of one series sweep.) To come home and make it four in a row would be too much, right?

Minnesota was in town, and the early answer seemed to be "yes." More than 42,000 fans at Comerica Park had to be figuring, "Here we go again." But then the offense exploded. Bobby Higginson ripped a two-run double in a four-run sixth inning. Suddenly, the Tigers were leading 4–3. Higgy would then add a two-run triple in the seventh, and the Tigers would blow it open and send the Opening Day crowd home happy with a 10–6 win.

Tiger Killers

Every team has them. It doesn't matter if we're talking about the best team in baseball or the cellar-dwellers. Every team has a group of opponents that just beat their brains in. It doesn't matter what time of the season, the score, or the situation. For whatever reason, these guys just never make an out and always come up with the big hit.

For some of these guys, it's pretty easy to figure out. They're All-Stars and Hall of Famers. I mean, nobody got Barry Bonds out. But there's also a group of average players who own certain teams. That's what makes baseball so great but so frustrating at the same time—ordinary guys can accomplish extraordinary feats.

So without further ado, here is my list of all-time, 100-percent-certified Tigers killers:

Jim Thome: There's no shame in having one of the preeminent sluggers of all time do some damage, but this is ridiculous. Whenever this giant of a man held his bat out with one hand, Tiger pitchers had to shiver with fear. Thome entered 2012 with 604 career home runs. It seems like about 600 of them were against the Tigers. He hit No. 599 and No. 600 in Detroit (in the same game!), and he now has 66 lifetime dingers against the Tigers. Here's some perspective for you—only Ted Williams (88), Mickey Mantle (73), Yogi Berra (72), and Harmon Killebrew (68) hit more homers against Detroit. It's hard to root against Thome because he's one of the nicest guys I've met in the game. But there weren't too many tears shed in Detroit when he signed with the Phillies in the National League.

Paul Konerko: Only Thome has more RBIs against the Tigers among active players. You want to know why it was so hard for us to beat the White Sox? Well, think about the fact that from 2006 to 2009, Thome and Konerko were on the *same team*. Paulie is also a standup guy who always has time for the media. That's probably because he knows he's going to rip your heart out that night.

Denard Span: The Twins have never been an easy opponent for the Tigers, no matter the record of either team. But it wasn't former MVP winners Justin Morneau and Joe Mauer who drove Tiger pitchers batty—it was Denard Span. From the moment he came up a few years ago, he has been a thorn in the Tigers paw. (You knew I had to say that at some point.) Span, now with the Washington Nationals, is a good player. Coming into 2014, his lifetime batting average was .283. But against Detroit, it was .346. Go figure.

Mark Grudzielanek: Not only could the Tigers not spell his name, but they couldn't get him out. The infielder didn't pack much power in his bat, but he hit .379 lifetime against Detroit.

Vlad Guerrero: Big Daddy Vladdy is going to the Hall of Fame. He terrorized many teams. Part of the reason is that there is no reasonable game plan on how to pitch this guy. I've seen him hit pitches that bounced as well as ones that are over his head. He swings at anything. And more often than not he connects, especially against the Tigers, as his .341 average can attest.

Shane Mack: Mack was a journeyman outfielder–designated hitter for the Twins, Red Sox, and Royals. Here's a surprising fact—he had a .299 lifetime average. A really surprising fact? He had a .376 average and a .449 on-base percentage against the Tigers.

Reggie Jefferson: Another surprising fact? Reggie Jefferson was a .300 lifetime hitter. But against the Tigers, he was .364.

Mr. Nice Guy

My first job broadcasting minor league baseball was in Peoria, Illinois. In many ways, Peoria is like most small Midwestern cities—a hard-working town where everyone is laid back and neighborly. I spent only two seasons working there, but the fans made me feel so much at home. Some of the nicest people I have met in my career are from Peoria.

The Minnesota Twins' Jim Thome swings for his 600th career home run during the seventh inning of a baseball game against the Detroit Tigers on Monday, August 15, 2011, in Detroit. *(AP Photo/Duane Burleson)*

It's no surprise that Jim Thome hails from Peoria. Thome has been one of baseball's most underappreciated sluggers from the mid-1990s through today. He's going to the Hall of Fame in my opinion. Even with that status, Jim always has time for the media. It doesn't matter if you're the announcer for his team or the Tigers, big market or small—he treats everyone the same. This guy is the personification of the old adage, "Treat people the way you'd like to be treated."

In my career, I've been blessed to call four no-hitters. But I had never been at the mic for a milestone accomplishment for a player. That's what made a 2011 series between the Tigers and Twins special.

The Tigers were in the midst of running away with the American League Central Division title. The Twins were dragging on their way to 99 losses. Their designated hitter was Thome, who was sitting on 598 career home runs.

Even though Thome was 40 years old, fighting a worn-out back and injured quad, you had to figure there was a pretty good chance he would join the 600 club at some point in the three-game series. If there was ever a certified Tiger-killer, it was Jim Thome.

During his career, Thome had gone deep 64 times against Detroit, and 15 of them occurred in Comerica Park. His batting stance was one of the most recognizable in the game. Holding the bat straight at the pitcher, he looked like a modern-day Babe Ruth.

On this mid-August night, Thome was in the lineup against ground-ball specialist Rick Porcello. It didn't seem to be a matchup made for history. But in the sixth inning, the Paul Bunyan lookalike smashed a two-run shot off Porcello for No. 599. We were on the doorstep of a special moment.

Thome came to bat again in the seventh, with the Twins leading 6–5. Left-handed flamethrower Daniel Schlereth was now on the hill. It didn't matter who was pitching, however, because this was Thome's moment. He deposited the ball over the left-field wall, becoming just the eighth player to join the 600 club.

I was trying to document history without sounding like I was rooting for the Twins. But the fact is that on this one occasion, I was rooting for Thome.

Probably the biggest statement about the man came as he crossed home plate. Tigers fans, who had watched Thome kill their team over and over again throughout the years, gave the slugger a standing ovation.

Having the chance to be part of history is something I'll never forget. It was the night that Jim Thome proved another old adage—good things happen to good people.

Mr. Nice Guy 2

When the Tigers signed Torii Hunter prior to the 2013 season, they knew they were getting a nine-time Gold Glove outfielder. They also knew they were getting a guy who was on the verge of 2,000 hits and 300 home runs. But more than anything, they knew they were getting one of the best clubhouse guys in all of baseball. Still, after spending some time with Torii, I realized that even the most optimistic reports still underrated his character.

When Torii arrived in Lakeland for spring training, it wasn't like he was a stranger to any of us. Having spent nine years with the division rival Twins, then another five with the Angels, Tiger players obviously knew him well. Most of the media knew him, too. Having said that, I still found myself a little bit in awe of just how good a guy he is.

Considering his childhood, the fact that Torii has turned out the way he did is nothing short of amazing. Pine Bluff, Arkansas, is a rough town. So rough that it has been labeled the most dangerous "little town" in America. A city of roughly 49,000 people, violence is a way of life, and the town's infrastructure has not been updated in years.

It is also Hunter's home town.

That Torii has overcome the long odds to carve out a borderline Hall of Fame career is impressive enough. The way that he's turned out as a person is even more amazing. When I asked him how this happened, the Tigers right fielder broke into a smile.

"I know where I come from," Hunter said. "I've had family problems—my father was a drug addict—but at the same time, you would never know. I put a smile on my face, and I'm thankful for the chance to put on a major league uniform every day."

That smile has carried Hunter through a lot of tough times growing up, but he never let on that things were not easy.

"We didn't have much. A lot of times the electricity was cut off, and we were hungry. My grandmother always told me not to let anybody see you down and depressed, and I try to carry myself the right way."

Even today, whether he's 10 for his last 20 or 0-for-10, Torii is a guy who's happy to be living the life he has. In a marathon of more than 162 games, that is invaluable.

Hunter is one of the best defensive center fielders of his generation. Only six outfielders have won more than his nine Gold Gloves. Yet when the Angels twice had young center fielders come up—Peter Bourjous and Mike Trout—Torii graciously moved to right. And he didn't pout. Instead, he shared his knowledge with the youngsters. This was one of the reasons he came to Detroit.

"I'm going to be in Austin Jackson's ear every day. I've been through everything, and I'm going to help him learn about being a great center fielder."

Wherever he has played, Hunter has quickly earned the respect of those around him. When the Tigers opened a three-game series in Anaheim in April 2013, Hunter received a standing ovation from the Angels fans in attendance. You don't normally see that for an opposing player, especially one who only spent five seasons there.

"It was really cool," Hunter said. "The standing ovation was kind of like my grade for my time in Anaheim. I guess it showed that the fans there appreciated the way I play the game."

It's an appreciation that Tigers fans are quickly gaining, as well.

Prince and Miggy

In January 2012, the Tigers received some potentially devastating news. Designated hitter Victor Martinez had been injured during off-season workouts and tore his ACL, apparently ending his season before it even started.

The longtime Cleveland Indian and former Boston Red Sox had signed with Detroit the previous winter, helping to lead the Tigers to their first division title in 24 years. On the field, Victor did more than his part, hitting .330

with 103 RBI and providing Miguel Cabrera with much-need protection in the lineup.

In the clubhouse, V-Mart was even more valuable. His veteran experience and winning attitude brought stability that the team would need during a long season. This loss would be tough to recover from.

Tigers owner Mike Ilitch has always been known for making bold moves, and this was no different. About a week later, the Tigers struck—and in a huge way.

Ilitch reached deep into his pockets and signed Prince Fielder, the free agent first baseman formerly of the Milwaukee Brewers. The price tag was steep—nine years and $214 million—but it was clear that the 2012 Tigers were leaving no stone unturned.

The team also announced that Prince would play first base while Miguel Cabrera would return to third base. As an announcer, I look at trades or signings in two ways. First, what does it mean for the team? How will he fit in? Does it make the team better? The second thing I ponder is a little more selfish. How does it affect me and the rest of the local media? Prince, of course, is the son of former Tigers All-Star Cecil Fielder. The two were reportedly not on the best of terms, and Prince had a reputation in the media as a tough interview.

Fast-forward a couple of weeks to the eve of spring training when I got a call from FOX Sports Detroit Executive Producer John Tuohey, who asked me if I'd be interested in doing a joint interview with Prince and Cabrera to air as a *Tigers Weekly* episode.

I was stunned. With Miguel, I was not surprised. As he has become more comfortable in Detroit, he has really let down his guard and showed more of his personality. But to have the opportunity to sit down both of these superstars? Wow.

Once I got to Lakeland, Brian Britten, the Tigers' public relations director at the time, introduced me to Prince. Right away, I could see that my preconception was not accurate. I thanked Prince for agreeing to do the interview and he said, "No problem. Anything you need." It wasn't so much what he said as much as how he said it. This was going to be a really cool experience.

So on a hot 85-degree day, I headed out to the back fields at TigerTown, where the interview would be shot after the Tigers finished that day's game. Now granted, this was spring training—the games didn't count, and players only play a few innings. But I was still a little nervous about how things would go.

This, too, ended up being a case of worrying about nothing. Not only did the interview go well, but it was actually fun. I was really struck by how comfortable the two new teammates were around each other. They laughed throughout the whole thing, punching each other and making jokes. These two superstars felt like they had been together for years.

I don't know if this was the most accomplished duo I had ever sat with, but between the Prince and Miggy, we're talking about more than 600 home runs and 13 All-Star Games. The interview proved worthy of two of the best players in the game.

Legends Among Us

One of the most important things about baseball, if not the most important, is its history. This is how fans of all ages make a connection. It's how children learn about the game. In my experience, this is also an area that many teams can improve upon.

Every team has iconic players who define their franchise. Think about Stan "The Man" Musial and the St. Louis Cardinals, the "Splendid Splinter" Ted Williams and the Boston Red Sox, and Mickey Mantle (among others) and the New York Yankees. I think teams need to do a better job of celebrating their pasts.

The Tigers honor their greats on the brick outfield wall and with statues in center field. But what's really cool about working at Comerica Park is that if you hang around the ballpark long enough, there's a great chance you'll run into two of the Tigers greats in person—Al Kaline and Willie Horton. These guys show how important it is to utilize your legends.

I was a little too young to see Kaline in his prime. Mr. Tiger was one of the game's great right fielders. Al's glory days were in the 1950s and 1960s when he was on his way to racking up 399 career home runs. He played in 16

All-Star Games and won 10 Gold Gloves. He was elected to baseball's Hall of Fame in 1980 with one of the highest percentages in history.

It's always a thrill to talk to Al about what the game was like during his era and how the city embraced the team. Listening to him is like opening a vault of Detroit and Tigers history. He has seen it all, from world championships to the American League's losingest team. More importantly, he's done it all, from a Hall of Fame playing career to being a broadcaster and now a special assistant to Dave Dombrowski.

He may be 79 years old, but when he's around the batting cage or in the clubhouse, he's like a kid again. I think Al really enjoys sharing his advice and wisdom (but only when asked) with the players of today.

One of Kaline's All-Star teammates was Willie Horton. If you want local, then Willie is your guy. He went to Detroit Northwestern High School and spent 14 of his 18 big-league seasons with the Tigers. His mark on the team is obvious, but his imprint on the community is even greater.

Horton took to the streets of Detroit (while in uniform!) to try to calm the city during the 1967 riots. Imagine that for a second—a major league player in uniform, risking his life during race riots. That's all you need to know about the character of Willie Horton.

Oh, he could play, too. Willie pounded 325 home runs and is best known for throwing out Lou Brock at home plate during Game 5 of the 1968 World Series.

In an age when so many athletes are unapproachable, there's no one warmer than Willie. One of my favorite parts of the job is passing Willie in the press box or on the field. He always has a big smile, and he extends his hand, asking in his booming voice, "Whaddya say, son? How ya doin' today?"

Even at 71 years young, Willie lives and dies for his Tigers. One of my lasting impressions of this big hulking man was interviewing him in the locker room in Kansas City in 2006 after the Tigers had beaten the Royals to clinch a playoff spot for the first time in 19 years.

I remember asking him what this playoff clincher meant to the city in a postgame interview from the clubhouse.

"You're a Detroiter," he told me. "You know what it means to the people of this town. It's unbelievable."

Horton was known as one of the toughest players to play the game, but on this day he was nearly in tears as he spoke about how proud he was of the Tigers and what the victory had done for the city.

Having Kaline and Horton around the ballpark is an important part of keeping the Tigers' rich history alive.

Trading Places

Every baseball season has four major mile markers in my opinion. Spring training is the unofficial New Year's for baseball. We've all been freezing for months, watching hockey and begging to go outside. Players are tired of indoor workouts and want to play some real baseball. Rookies are eager to impress the coaching staff, and the older players are ready to get going. For me, there's nothing like those first few days where old acquaintances are renewed and you get to meet the new faces. Snowbirds migrate to either Florida or Arizona. Everyone can see the light at the end of the tunnel.

Then there's Opening Day. By now, the guys are really ready to go. There's such a sense of renewal. Everyone is undefeated, and every team has a chance. The possibilities are endless. I love the pageantry and the excitement. Nothing that happened before that matters because the whole season is in front of us.

The postseason, of course, is the best time. We're about to watch a new champion get crowned, and the intensity is unmatched. Every pitch is the end of the world, and everyone is on the edge of his or her seat.

Then there is perhaps the most anticipated marker—the July 31 non-waiver trading deadline. It doesn't matter whether your team is in first or last place, everyone is involved. Are you a buyer or a seller? Who's on the market? Now granted, only about 25 percent of the rumored deals actually happen, but it doesn't dim the excitement at all.

One of the big challenges for general managers around the game is fighting the temptation to make a deal just for the sake of making a deal. It's a good thing that they don't pay attention to the fans. Like the saying goes, if you listen to the fans too often, you'll become one.

Baseball history is littered with moves that haven't worked out. For example, the Red Sox traded future All-Star Jeff Bagwell to Houston for middle reliever Larry Andersen. Another example is when the Tigers dealt future Hall of Famer John Smoltz to the Braves for Doyle Alexander. I really shouldn't say those trades didn't work out at all—they were just a case of short-term gain for long-term pain.

Successful GMs have a few rules when it comes to making trades. First, trade with people you respect. Second, trust the opinions of your scouts. And third, know your own prospects.

These rules apply to both off-season and deadline deals. And nobody has done a better job over the last few winters than Dave Dombrowski and the Tigers.

In the winter of 2007, the two top Tigers prospects were outfielder Cameron Maybin and pitcher Andrew Miller. They were both first-round picks and considered by outsiders to be untouchable. That, however, was not the case.

The Tigers realized that Maybin had some holes in his swing and Miller might not be able to consistently throw strikes in the big leagues. Dombrowski was able to deal the perceived value of both prospects to Florida for Miguel Cabrera and Dontrelle Willis. While Willis provided the Tigers with a grand total of (count them) two wins in parts of three seasons in Detroit, Cabrera made the deal a win. Huge advantage Tigers.

In 2009, a three-team deal sent fan favorite Curtis Granderson to the Yankees and netted leadoff man Austin Jackson and Phil Coke from New York plus 21-game winner and All-Star Max Scherzer from Arizona.

Some of Dombrowski's deadline deals haven't grabbed as much attention, but without them, the Tigers wouldn't have made the playoffs.

There was a hole at first base late in the 2006 season. Chris Shelton had come back to Earth after a historic start, and the Tigers needed someone they could depend on. Veteran Sean Casey was finishing an injury-plagued season with the perennially disappointing Pittsburgh Pirates. The cost was pretty cheap—minor league pitcher Brian Rogers, who ended up pitching in 13 big-league games. Casey solidified the infield, and the Tigers went to the World Series.

Nobody noticed in 2010 when the Tigers dealt minor league lefty Giovanni Soto to Cleveland for Jhonny Peralta. Dombowski knew he needed a replacement for the struggling Brandon Inge, but Peralta seemed to be an underwhelming choice.

This one didn't pay instant dividends, as the Tigers finished third, but Peralta emerged the next season, earning his first All-Star berth and helping Detroit win its first division title in 24 years.

In that 2011 season, the GM was at it again, dealing three young players to Seattle for a relatively unknown 6'8" pitcher with a record of 3–12. Doug Fister clearly just needed a change of scenery because he went 8–1 down the stretch for the division winners and was a stalwart until being traded to Washington following the 2013 season.

In 2012 the Miami Marlins were once again looking to deal established players for prospects. This time, it was pitcher Anibal Sanchez and former Tiger Omar Infante. The price was a group of minor leaguers led by former first-round pick Jacob Turner.

Sanchez became a huge clutch performer in the playoffs, and Infante turned into the second baseman the team had been lacking since the departure of Placido Polanco, a previous mid-season deal. An uneven season turned into a World Series appearance.

The art of the deal is one that Dombrowski has certainly mastered.

Making the Most of a Moment

Broadcasting for nearly 10 years in the minor leagues has given me an appreciation for how difficult this game can be, both on the field and behind the mic.

When I first started, I thought everyone on every team was a future bigleaguer. Think about it—nearly all of these guys were the best player on their teams growing up, ranging from little league to travel ball, from high school and in some cases to college.

That's one of the reasons I get upset when fans refer to certain players as a scrub. That "scrub" has more baseball talent than about 99 percent of the world. The problem in the minors, of course, is that they're competing with players of the same or better abilities, so it's hard to really stand out.

My years of broadcasting in the minors taught me what separates good players from great ones. It's not how far you hit the ball or how fast you throw—it comes down to what's between the ears. There's no question that the equalizer is the mental part of the game.

We hear about basketball players who were streetball legends but never made it in the NBA. Baseball is the same way. I've seen many players who hit long home runs at a dizzying rate but could never rise above Triple A. If I had a dollar for every pitcher I saw with the million-dollar arm but 10-cent head syndrome…well, I'd be a millionaire.

Everyone who gets a chance to play professionally has talent, but there are obviously different levels of talent. Sure, everyone notices the Miguel Cabreras and Justin Verlanders, but a lot of major league players are just average prospects who keep working until it's their time to shine.

That's why I've always admired guys who toil away in the minors, making the most of their opportunities. The 2012 Tigers had a guy who is perseverance personified, and his name was Quintin Berry.

On a team with guys like Cabrera, Verlander, and Prince Fielder, you could still make an argument that without a minor league vagabond nicknamed "Q," the Tigers would have had a more difficult time making the postseason.

In mid-May, Austin Jackson landed on the disabled list with an abdominal injury. Talk about bad timing. A-Jax was batting .331 at the time.

Berry was signed by the Tigers as insurance for Austin Jackson. Good thing. When Jackson went down in May, Berry was called to the big leagues.

After 6½ years and nearly 700 games in the minor leagues, the San Diego native was hanging out in a big-league clubhouse for the first time in his career.

Berry made his first impression during spring training in 2012 when he collected big hit after big hit. His speed also opened some eyes, along with his whatever-it-takes attitude.

In the booth one day in the middle of camp, Rod Allen turned to me and said, "This guy is going to make the team." I agreed. Of course, the next day Berry was sent down. Timing is not our strong suit.

Berry was naturally discouraged when he was sent down, but he didn't let his disappointment show. He thought about the sacrifices he had made, taking jobs like working at the front desk of a 24-Hour Fitness. He decided he was not ready to give up.

So when Jackson was injured, Berry became what he had always dreamed of—a major leaguer. It immediately became clear that Q wasn't going to let this opportunity pass him by. In his third at-bat, he made his mark with a bunt double just over the infield. Think about that. Quintin waited all this time to get his shot, and he bunted for a double for his first hit!

Berry was exactly the lightning bolt of energy the team needed, hitting better than .300 for his first 35 games. His enthusiasm helped the Tigers absorb the loss of their center fielder. Quintin defied the odds and stuck with the club for the rest of the season.

I don't know what the future holds for Quintin Berry, but I do know that he'll always have 2012, the year he finally got his opportunity.

The Real Sparky

There's no question that the most difficult position on the diamond, at least physically, is behind the plate. After all, their equipment has been called the "tools of ignorance."

Through the years, Tigers fans have had a tremendous opportunity to see some of the best catchers of the era. We've had everything from Hall of Famer Mickey Cochrane to future Hall of Famer Pudge Rodriguez. In fact, the Tigers have had an All-Star catcher in the 1960s (Bill Freehan), the 1970s (Freehan again), the 1980s (Lance Parrish), the 1990s (Mickey Tettleton), the 2000s (Pudge), and now the 2010s (Alex Avila). That's pretty impressive.

All of these guys were very good hitters, and some were great behind the plate. But nobody has the special ability that Avila has—the ability to attract debilitating foul tips.

What's interesting is that Alex never planned on being a catcher. He comes from an impressive family history in the game, and his dad, Al, is the Tigers' assistant general manager.

Alex played first and third base during his high school career and at the University of Alabama. Heading into Alex's junior year, his coach approached him about changing positions because the Tide needed help behind the plate.

Few people would have predicted Avila would be a major league catcher after just 1½ seasons in the minors. Few people would have seen him as an All-Star in just his second full season in the bigs. And nobody could have anticipated the amount of abuse he would take behind the dish.

All catchers know that the position is physically demanding, but I've never seen anyone take the amount of foul tips that Alex has. His fingers, his feet, his knees, his chest—no place is safe. This doesn't include collisions at the plate, either. Avila even suffered concussion-like symptoms when his chin knocked into Prince Fielder's elbow while chasing a pop foul. As you can imagine, Alex dropped like a prize fighter.

Yet with all of these incidents, one stands out. It is something I have never seen before in broadcasting more than 2,800 professional baseball games.

In a September 2011 game in Chicago, Avilia took a foul tip off his mask. But this was no ordinary foul tip. We've heard about balls being hit so hard that you can almost see sparks. Well, this one—which came off the bat of A.J. Pierzynski—drilled Avila so hard that sparks actually flew off his mask. "It was like a firecracker coming off my mask," Avila recalled. Stunningly, Alex was uninjured.

Perhaps the funniest part is that initially Alex had no idea it even happened. During the telecast, we had great slow-motion replay that really showed the sparks flying off the mask. On the bus back to the hotel, I pulled out my phone and showed him a video that had already started to make its rounds on the Internet. His helmet looked like the 4th of July.

The next day at the park, it was all everyone was talking about. It was something nobody had ever seen.

The Tiger–White Sox rivalry has been a good one over the years, but this was one instance when sparks were literally flying.

———

We've already established which position on the field takes the most

Alex Avila (13) during a game against the Toronto Blue Jays on April 9, 2013, at Comerica Park in Detroit, Michigan. The Tigers beat the Blue Jays 7–3. *(AP Photo/ David Durochik)*

abuse. Aside from foul tips, there are the occasional collisions at the plate that can end a player's season. (Just ask San Francisco's Buster Posey.)

Clearly, foul tips are becoming more of an issue in Major League Baseball. They happen every game, and most of the time we don't even notice them. But ask any veteran catcher, and he'll show you disfigured fingers, bruises, and other aches and pains that were caused from these seemingly harmless foul tips. And this doesn't take into account the thousands upon thousands of times they squat and get up, squat and get up.

This is one of the reasons I get frustrated when fans criticize a catcher's offensive production without taking the entire picture into consideration. As great as Mike Piazza was with a bat in his hands, think about how much better he would have been if he didn't miss an average of 40 games a season because he was catching.

Look at Johnny Bench, generally considered one of the top three catchers in baseball history. The Reds used him at first and third base later in his career, and he was still out of the game at age 35. Piazza played until he was 39, but his resistance to learn first base probably cost him another couple of years, plus a chance at 500 home runs. (He finished with 427.)

There's no question that catching is like dog years for a player's career. That's why having a great one means so much.

When the Tigers brought up Alex Avila in 2009, there were snickers of nepotism because his father was the Tigers' assistant GM. After a disappointing rookie year, however, Alex proved his worth with an All-Star berth in his second season, helping lead the Tigers to the American League Central title. But even in the second half of that season, I could see the bumps and bruises were taking a toll.

If it weren't for bad luck, some guys would have no luck at all. Alex has taken his share of foul tips to the head, arm, shoulders, knees, legs, and everywhere in between. It seems like every night, Avila is hammered by a foul tip that buckles him to the ground. Yet it's a series of direct hits to the face-mask—both from foul tips and collisions—that has raised some concerns for the future health of all catchers, not just Avila. In 2013 alone, Avila, John Jaso (A's), and David Ross (Red Sox), plus All-Stars Joe Mauer (Twins) and Salvador Perez (Royals), all spent time on the concussion list.

Football was the first sport to really focus in on the effects of concussions, but now baseball and all other major sports are starting to pay more attention. Dizziness, headaches, and nausea have been the chief symptoms for Avila in his battle with these concussions, but it's the long-term affects that have medical personnel concerned for athletes.

Avila represents the third generation of baseball players in his family. He knows the risks, but his stay on the concussion list has him thinking more about his future and his family's future, especially after his first child was born.

"It's been on my mind a lot," Avila said. "When I saw pictures of my daughter on the road, or when I was in Toledo and I had to come out of the first [rehab] game, I'm not going to lie—it was on my mind. But at the same time, I know that there are people who care about me as far as making sure that I am healthy."

The attention paid to concussions is relatively new. When the A's were town in 2013, I chatted with Oakland TV analyst Ray Fosse, who played in the big leagues for 12 years.

Fosse was a two-time All-Star and two-time Gold Glove winner, but he's best remembered for being on the wrong end of the famous Pete Rose collision at home plate in the 1970 Midsummer Classic.

Back in his day, collisions at the plate were far more prevalent, but Ray also took his share of foul tips during his career. So what was the difference?

"We were never tested for concussions back then, but looking back now I'm sure I suffered a few. We just played," Fosse remembered. "After a collision or foul tip, players used to tell me, 'Foss, your eyes look like slot machines.' We took just as many shots, but today they test for it."

Fosse even played in an era where catching equipment was quite primitive compared to today's standards.

"I used to wear a soft cap at the beginning of my career," he said. "If you got hit on a backswing, we didn't have a helmet. You learned to position yourself so it wouldn't happen.

"The equipment has gotten much better. My mask was so short, I used to get cut under the chin from foul balls all the time."

In the late 1970s, a freak injury to Dodgers catcher Steve Yeager proved that necessity is truly the mother of invention.

Yeager was in the on-deck circle when batter Bill Russell shattered his bat. Yeager had no chance to react, and nine pieces of wood lodged in his esophagus.

Miraculously, Yeager survived after 90 minutes of surgery. But when he returned, Dodgers trainer Bill Buhler invented a piece of plastic that would hang from Yeager's mask to protect his throat. Most catchers today, whatever style of mask they wear, have that throat protector.

As Ray Fosse was talking about his primitive equipment, there was no bravado or bitterness; it was simply a different time. Unfortunately for him, today's medical technology was not available. If they would have had MRIs in his era, his entire career may have been different. After the Rose collision, doctors would have diagnosed his fractured and separated shoulder immediately. He probably would have had surgery, or at the very least he would have had some rest. Instead, he waited for the pain to subside and continued to play through it. He was never the same player, and he was out of the game by age 32.

Thankfully, with medical advances and the size of player contracts, the attention to injuries has become acute. I'm sure things still get missed, but in most cases, discretion is the better part of valor.

Alex Avila is still a young man in his mid-twenties with most of his career (not to mention his life) still ahead of him, but he's obviously concerned about the beating he takes. I asked Fosse if the sheer amount of foul tips Avila takes are a coincidence or related in any way to the staff he catches.

"Just bad luck," Fosse said.

Maybe the tools of ignorance should be renamed the tools of bravery.

View from the Studio

If I had to choose, I would say 2006, 2011, 2012, and 2013 have probably been the best four years of my broadcasting career because the Tigers—the team I cover and the team I grew up loving—have advanced to postseason play. In some ways, this is a double-edged sword, both personally and professionally.

Of course I always want the Tigers to do well. Both as a broadcaster and a fan, it makes the summer that much more enjoyable to see them playing so well.

Incidentally, this is one of the big differences between my job and working for, say, FOX Network or ESPN. Those broadcasters may have teams they like, but really, they're just rooting for good storylines. That's why it's so funny when fans complain that the national announcers don't like this team or they don't want a team to advance. If there's a compelling story, it doesn't matter who is playing.

But for me, we are with the Tigers for more than 150 games each year. We fly with them, stay in the same hotels, and get to know the players fairly well. And from a business standpoint, if the team is hot, ratings rise. If ratings rise, we all benefit. (The Tigers in 2012 delivered the highest ratings of any team in the entire major leagues.) So of course we have a vested interest.

What makes the playoffs bittersweet is that, on the TV side, we aren't doing the games. Dan Dickerson and Jim Price get to broadcast the postseason on radio all the way up until the final pitch. But our television broadcast team is replaced by either TBS, the MLB Network, or FOX.

Naturally, we would rather be in the booth, broadcasting every game, but at least the postseason lets us really think like fans. The challenge for us is how to best cover the playoffs without being the actual rights holder.

This is something management at FOX Sports Detroit really spends a lot of time thinking about before coming up with a plan. And each year, we've been able to do a little bit more.

In the last couple of postseasons, in particular, I think we've found a good working model. For home games, I head down to Comerica Park and help out there. I might be doing occasional interviews, or I might be sharing some thoughts with John Keating.

Our auxiliary press area is either in the left- or right-field stands. It can certainly get cold, but hey, we're at the game, right? I'll sit with a host of producers and reporters, and the neat thing is that we get to share observations and pick each other's brains, which definitely adds to the viewing experience.

During the Tigers' march to the 2012 World Series, though, I had several writers comment to me about how fidgety and nervous I looked in our press area while I was sitting and watching the games. Rod Allen and Craig Monroe stayed in the studio to share their analysis with a host, usually Mickey York. This has given us a nice balance—almost a full-court press on the big games.

On road games, all three of us are in the studio, watching the game on TV, just like you do at home. And, yes, we yell at the screen, just like you!

While I'd rather be broadcasting the games, watching them provides a very different perspective. Behind the mic, you get the feeling of control, although we obviously have no impact on what happens. Watching either in person or on TV, it feels totally hopeless. It is so nerve-racking that it almost feels like we actually played the game.

One of the fun parts of watching the games in studio is that it's almost like being at a sports bar. We can first-guess, second-guess, and talk about different possibilities a lot more freely than we could if we were actually broadcasting. That exchange of ideas can really pay off, too.

In Game 2 of the 2012 World Series, all Tigers fans remember the play when third-base coach Gene Lamont sent Prince Fielder home on a base hit to left. It turned out to be a bad decision; the Giants' Marco Scutaro made a perfect catch and throw to the plate, and Buster Posey made a perfect tag.

Rod, Craig, and I all had a different take on what had happened. Rod pointed out that Lamont should have been further down the baseline to get a better view of the left fielder. Craig pointed out that Jhonny Peralta should have instructed Prince to slide to the inside part of the plate. I broke down the heads-up play by Scutaro who, as the double-cut man, was in the perfect spot for an overthrow, and of course he made the precise throw. One play with three perspectives for the viewers. The collaboration made the telecast that much better.

One thing about any telecast is that there are usually funny, behind-the-scenes things going on. It's kind of like a hot dog—you like the final product, but you don't always want to know how it's made.

Naturally, we would all rather be doing the game, but the atmosphere in the studio is pretty funny, too. We all sit there with our notebooks, cell phones, and either our iPads or laptops. It seems like just about every play causes someone to look up something on their device. It might be a stat, a rule, or even some type of point to settle an argument. Like I said, it can be like a sports bar in there.

We get out to the set in the ninth inning so we can get on the air as soon as the game ends. This can provide more funny moments. Sometimes I think the better action would be to have a camera on us to watch our reactions. We'll slam the desk, bury our heads in our hands, or even give high fives. You might expect those reactions from me and Mickey, but Rod and Craig played in the majors, so it's great for them to feel the emotions like us fans.

Once we hit the air, it's like our playoff game. In pregame, things are scripted—it's just a matter of execution. But in postgame, we're flying without a net.

We never know which interview we're going to hear, so we really have to listen. Especially with Jim Leyland because he can say just about anything. What we thought was a meaningless play in the fourth inning may be something he focuses on in the postgame interview.

Then we come on air and have to react. The adrenaline of the postgame show is an incredible rush. A lot of times we get off the set after the show and have no idea if we made any sense or not. It's that intense.

CHAPTER 5
GAME DAY

It's All in the Prep

One of the most underrated but critical aspects of broadcasting is preparation. There has long been a misconception that we show up an hour before game time, put on our jackets and ties, and it's time to play. In reality, nothing could be further from the truth.

One of the really cool things about my job is that I'm preparing, even when I don't realize it. Being a huge baseball fan, it seem like I'm always watching a game on TV or reading about one. Yes, that counts as prep work. If I was an accountant or a lawyer, I'd still be a huge Tigers fan and want to know everything that's going on with the team.

At the risk of sounding even older than I am, kids today have no idea what it was like back in the mid-1980s, long before the Internet came around. The information highway was more like a slow trudge. The first thing I did each day as a minor league broadcaster was to come to the ballpark and wait for the league to fax over official stats from the night before. Sometimes they came, and sometimes they didn't. It was up to us to fill in the blanks and dig up info on a player's background.

These days, with the Internet and the myriad of stat and bio services available, broadcasters are like kids at Christmas. Need to know how Miguel Cabrera has done against CC Sabathia over his career? All it takes is a couple of clicks, and the answer is right there.

Today's technology also allows us to prep all year long. Baseball is so different from any other sport. The sheer volume of games and the fact that you will play the same team three straight nights and in some cases 18 or 19 times a year makes it challenging to keep things fresh. Invariably we'll be in Cleveland or Kansas City in September after having played them 15 times already, and there is just nothing fresh to say. I'll read a feature about some backup catcher on the Kansas City Royals in December, and during a mid-July game, it might come in handy.

Much like the players who have a pretty strict regimen for game day, here's my schedule for a 7:00 PM game.

9:00 AM: Top o' the morning! Wake up, have breakfast with my wife and sons (if they're home). Catch up on anything I might have missed from the previous 24 hours.

10:00 AM: Hit the gym and try to get in a workout. Obviously, that's easier on the road, but when you feel good physically, it's a lot easier to do a good job. Thanks to my iPad, this also gives me a chance to read the papers and catch up on what's going on.

11:30 AM: Morning chat with our game producer to see what we're thinking about for the broadcast. Sometimes the story is obvious, e.g., Justin Verlander coming off a 12-strikeout game, a huge matchup with the Yankees, etc.

12:30 PM: Grab some lunch, usually something light. My dinner will be early, so I don't want to fill up. Another good opportunity for spouse time.

2:45 PM: Off to the truck. This is a chance to say hello to the producer and director, and let them know that I have indeed shown up for work. We'll chat about any changes since we spoke in the morning and make sure we're all on the same page for that night's broadcast.

3:10 PM: Arrive in the booth and start filling out my score sheet.

3:30 PM: I'll work my way over to the manager's office to listen in on Jim Leyland's get-together. Just like the players, this is when you generally get to see the skipper "unplugged" in a casual environment. Jim feels totally at home in his office. He usually has a T-shirt on, no shoes, and he's smoking a cigarette. When he's relaxed like this, he speaks pretty frankly. The one thing he won't do is put up with an interviewer he feels hasn't done his homework. He eats those guys for lunch.

4:00 PM: It's over to the Tigers locker room. I try to be more of an observer here. If I have a question for player, this is a great time to ask it. Guys are generally pretty relaxed, and sometimes we'll make small talk before they take the field at 4:45 for batting practice. I make sure that I always make myself available in the locker room every day in the event that a player wants to talk about something I may have said on the broadcast. It doesn't happen often, but occasionally a player takes issue with something I may have said.

4:30 PM: Time for the long walk up. I'll make the trek up to the media room and hibernate in our broadcast booth to fill out my score sheet with line-ups and other miscellaneous information. Rod usually hangs out by the cage for batting practice, but for me, this is a good time to prepare some last-minute notes.

5:00 PM: Dinner time! We call this a working dinner. I'll sit with the producer, director, and crew, and we'll chat about whatever else needs to be addressed. Sometimes we just talk baseball or life. It's our last chance to decompress before we hit the air.

6:00 PM: The last look. Rod and I will meet in the booth and watch any video elements for the night's telecast. There might be highlights or interviews for us to check out. We'll also have a chance to rehearse our opening segment, which we'll do live. On occasion, one of us will appear on the *Tigers Live!* pregame show, which airs most nights at 6:00.

7:00 PM: The red light goes on, and it's game time.

Hey, You Got a Second?

They say that baseball is a game of inches, and that's true. But as a broadcaster, I've learned that it's also a game of minutes. Or in this case, five minutes. Here's how five measly minutes can be a harbinger of things to come.

The first pitch may be at 7:05 PM, but by then our day is halfway done.

For a night game, I usually arrive at the park by about 2:45 PM. This gives me a chance to listen in on the manager's press gathering. It's not really a press conference but more of an informal question-and-answer session. Some of the skipper's best stuff comes out here, in a very casual setting in his office.

Even if I don't end up using 90 percent of what is said, this is a great chance to get some insight into what Brad Ausmus—or when I was with the Angels, Mike Scoscia—is thinking. You never know when that little nugget of information will come in handy.

Once the manager is done, I'll spend a few minutes trolling the clubhouse, usually just making small talk with the players. Again, you never know what kind of information you'll gather. It may be as simple as asking a player about the game last night or about an injury or an upcoming opponent.

Then comes what should be the easiest part of the day—the pregame interview. When I was working on radio, this was an essential ingredient to the pregame show.

It really shouldn't be that hard. A player spends five minutes or less with me, and they're off to batting practice. But sometimes it's just not that easy.

I remember trying to interview Nomar Garciaparra when he was on the Red Sox. He said he'd talk with me "after he got dressed." That turned into "after he took early batting practice," which turned into "after regular batting practice." Finally, when he finished up, I approached him and asked him for five minutes. He told me he didn't have time for me. I got the feeling he never wanted to do it in the first place. I think he was just hoping I would go away. The funny thing is that I would have done just that had he been honest up front and said, "Not today."

In 1995, I was covering the California Angels. The closer on the team was Lee Smith. He was nearing the end of an All-Star career, one where he retired as baseball's all-time saves leader. Lee was a quiet guy who kept to himself. One day in July, I thought it would be a nice change of pace to hear from the big man in the pregame interview.

I asked Smith if he had a couple of minutes. He responded, "Who are you?" as if he had never seen me before.

"Seriously?" I replied.

"Yeah…don't know who you are," he said.

"I'm the guy who tells everybody how great you are every time you pitch."

Now granted, I wasn't his teammate, but I was the play-by-play voice, doing every single game, flying on the same team charter, riding the same bus to the park. You might think he'd at least recognize my face, right?

Let me say that, for the most part, this has not been a problem for me. The players know we have a job to do, and we're trying to portray them in a positive light. In fact, I've made up my best all-time pregame interview team. These are guys who "get it" and make our jobs easier:

1B: Mike Sweeney—He never turned me down.

2B: Rex Hudler—There was never a question he'd go into broadcasting.

3B: Brandon Inge—He always had time for me and a crazy quote.

LF: Garret Anderson—Garret was misunderstood because he was so quiet, but he always bailed me out.

CF: Torii Hunter—His reputation as a class act is well-deserved.

RF: Tim Salmon—Tim once turned me down because he had to hit, then he left his hitting session early because he felt bad.

C: Sandy Alomar Jr.—Being from a baseball family, Sandy understands the process.

DH: Jim Thome—Jim is simply the nicest guy I've met in the game.

P: Chuck Finley—He once did an interview for me at Tiger Stadium on the field. It started raining during the interview, but he wouldn't move until we finished.

Manager: Joe Maddon—Joe gave very intelligent, insightful answers.

Honorable mention Hall of Famer: Frank Robinson—My tape snapped in the middle of the interview, and he graciously waited for me to grab another cassette and we redid the interview. (Yes, I'm so old we actually used to use cassette tapes.)

Don't Judge a Book

The one thing I have learned about players in my 25-plus years of covering them is that you can't always believe what you hear.

Every player has a reputation—good or bad. Some of these reputations are deserved, while some are not. Like fans, sometimes broadcasters have preconceived notions of guys based on what happens on the field. But some of the most popular players end up being not so nice in person, and others who might seem arrogant turn out to be just fine.

Many times I have been told that certain players are unapproachable. Yet most of the time it turned out to be untrue. I think many times it's just a case of laziness by the reporter. You hear a guy is a jerk so you don't bother to find out for yourself. In my experience, the times that I've taken a chance, more times than not, it has paid off.

In 1995, I was a rookie broadcaster for the Angels, and we were playing a series in Oakland. I needed an interview for the pregame show. I told my colleagues that I was going to ask Mark McGwire if he would be willing to chat. Now this was before Big Mac turned into the 70-homer, national-phenomenon Mark McGwire, but he was still a pretty big name.

Mark was a guy who pretty much kept to himself. He was known for being difficult with the media. Another broadcaster heard that I was planning to interview him and said I was wasting my time because there was no way McGwire would do it.

I'm glad I didn't listen. I approached McGwire before batting practice, and he was very gracious, giving me a great five-minute interview. I brought the interview back up to the booth, and many of my colleagues were amazed I was able to pull it off. It was really the first time that I realized that some reputations are undeserved. (Or maybe I just caught him on a good day.)

Another guy with a reputation for being difficult was Roger Clemens. When Clemens first came on the scene, he did interviews all the time. But as he became "The Rocket," things changed. His last few years in Boston were average at best, and the team let him go when GM Dan Duquette famously said that Clemens was "in the twilight of his career." By the time Roger signed with Toronto, he had something to prove on the field, and his disposition had worsened off of it.

Roger Clemens was on his way to winning 20 games for the fourth time in his career in 1997 while pitching for the Blue Jays. The Rocket had restored his luster, and he did it with a chip on his shoulder.

I knew some people who had covered him in Boston, and they had always warned me that he would never do an interview. In fact, he was well-known for his battles with the media. The late *Boston Globe* columnist Will McDonough used to call Clemens the "Texas Con Man" because he had stolen money and not lived up to his contract. My friends told me it was a total waste of time to try and talk to this guy.

One night in Anaheim I decided to give it a shot anyway. Clemens not only did a nice interview, but it's one that I have saved to this day.

When the Tigers traded for Gary Sheffield before the 2007 season, his reputation was…well, let's just say he was known as a surly person. Sheffield had come up as a teenager with Milwaukee and always had a contentious relationship with the press.

I first met Gary during the offseason Tigers winter caravan that year. I had never had any interaction with him and was pleasantly surprised at how talkative and personable he was. As the season progressed, I found him to be very open and approachable all season. Gary didn't sugarcoat anything, so you had to be ready for his opinion, but whether you agreed or disagreed with him, you respected the fact that he took the time to talk.

With some athletes, like Sheffield, perhaps they just mature as they get older and become easier to talk to. But I generally have found most guys are approachable. The one thing they want is to feel like you know what you're talking about. It doesn't mean they agree with what you're saying, but they need to respect your knowledge. I've seen many reporters chewed up by asking what the player or manager perceives to be a stupid question. Know your stuff, and they'll usually be cooperative.

Wait a Second. We're Live?

I'll never forget my first assignment with FOX Sports Detroit as the Tigers play-by-play voice. It was a spring training game, and my regular partner, Kirk Gibson, wasn't available, so we brought in Tom "Wimpy" Paciorek to fill in.

Tom is a great guy who gutted his way through an 18-year major league career in which he was a solid role player. Looking back, he was exactly the right guy to work with because I was so nervous doing my first Tigers game, and Wimpy is very laid back and funny. In fact, Wimpy actually relaxed me a bit since it was my first broadcast for the Tigers.

It was a night game at Joker Marchant Stadium, and even though we were in Lakeland, Florida, it can still get pretty cool at night. Normally during spring training, we are more relaxed and wear golf shirts, but not on this night. It was one of the few exhibition games I've ever done in a coat and tie.

Wimpy was so cold, he actually showed up wearing multiple T-shirts under his dress shirt, tie, and jacket. I didn't know what was funnier—that a guy who played nearly 20 years in the majors couldn't handle a little cold, or that he looked like the Michelin Man! The good news is that it was so hilarious that it actually relaxed me.

Many broadcasts will tape the opening segment with the two announcers. At FS Detroit, we believe in doing them live. There is always more energy that way.

Of course, doing them live carries some risk. Like on this night when radio voice Dan Dickerson decided he wanted to wish me good luck on my first broadcast. Dan had no idea we were on the air live. He came running down the press box, sliding across the floor like Tom Cruise in *Risky Business*. He eventually skidded to a stop in front of our booth. Realizing we were actually on the air, a look of horror came over his face. As for me, my concentration was shot. I stumbled through the opening and figured, "Wow, our viewers must be thinking, *Who is this goof?*"

———

July 5, 2002, seemed like any other mid-summer road game. The Tigers were in Boston to play the Red Sox. Earlier that day I had spoken with our producer Mark "Iceman" Iacofano about what we would cover in our game's opening segment.

When I arrived at Fenway Park, all our plans changed. Red Sox legend Ted Williams had passed away that day. NESN, the Red Sox–owned network was scrambling, but at least they had all the video they could possibly need. Our crew had only Tigers footage, so we were facing a daunting task to try to produce a fitting tribute for the greatest hitter of all time. And we were about three hours away from game time.

With our backs against the wall, Iceman did an incredible job, and we had a nice, long feature. It was well produced with black and white highlights and dramatic music, and it ended with a shot of the No. 9 cut into the outfield grass at Fenway.

Tom Paciorek was again filling in for Kirk Gibson as my partner again that night. Strange stuff always seems to happen when Wimpy fills in. When we came on camera for our opening shot following the somber video, the drama really started. I realized the flag on my microphone was upside down. Can you say "mood killer?" We were toast. How could we be respectful now? I looked like a fool with my mic flag upside down.

Iceman noticed the gaffe and quickly got us off camera by rolling some video of Williams. Meanwhile he got in my ear and told me to lose my mic and share Paciorek's mic. The problem was that Ice never told Tom of his plan.

So as Wimpy was talking and the video was playing, I begin leaning toward him to share his mic. He had no idea what was going on. In fact, he had to be wondering why I was getting so close to him that I was basically in his lap. It looked like I was whispering sweet nothings in his ear.

We stumbled our way through the rest of the segment, ruining what we felt was going to be a powerful opening.

As we went to commercial, the stage manager, whose job description includes putting the mic flags on correctly, looked at me and said, "Boy, that was funny."

I erupted. "Funny? Are you kidding me? You thought that was funny?"

I wanted to jump out of the booth and take her with me. Predictably she has not worked one of our telecasts since.

Sometimes it pays to tape the opening.

Together, But Separate

The dynamic between any play-by-play announcer and his color analyst is unique. From March through September, we spend more time together than we do with our spouses. You might think that would make us inseparable. But in reality, the relationship with your broadcast partner is rather complex.

In Detroit, I have worked with two color analysts—Rod Allen and Kirk Gibson. Rod played in the big leagues for parts of three seasons with three different teams. He also spent time playing in Japan, scouting and coaching in the minors. His baseball experience is broad.

Gibby's background is well known in Detroit and around baseball. He belted two of the most clutch home runs in World Series history—one against Goose Gossage and the Padres in 1984 and, of course, one against Dennis Eckersley in 1988. ("I can't believe what I just saw.") Both homers are a big part of World Series lore. Gibson coached for the Tigers and Diamondbacks, and in 2011 he was named the NL Manager of the Year, leading Arizona to an unlikely division title.

Even with their different experiences and accomplishments, both Rod and Kirk know the game inside and out. I can promise you that I have learned plenty about baseball from both men.

The main thing Rod, Kirk, and I have in common is our love of baseball. Rod and Kirk inherently have closer relationships with players because they played in the big leagues. My relationship with the players is more business-like in nature, for the most part.

The point is that we're different people with different professional backgrounds. Having never played baseball beyond high school, I can't relate to how difficult the game can be at the big-league level. However, having spent the early years of my professional career and ten years in the minor leagues learning the business, I can bring that broadcasting experience and background to the telecast.

On game days, we don't spend as much time together as most people would think. If we're home, I usually try to have breakfast and/or lunch with my wife and kids. My wife, Cathy, is a perfect partner for me. For my entire career, she's dealt with a part-time husband, but she never complains and has done an incredible job raising our two boys, Brett and Daniel.

I try to get in a workout before coming to the park. It's obviously easier to do when I'm on the road because I'm by myself, but when you sit as much as I do, it's important to get in some physical activity.

Before I head off to the ballpark, the rest of my time is spent researching. I try to read as much as possible, including the other team's local newspaper and any other baseball sites. This is where the Internet has been such a dramatic help. Before last season, some of my cohorts convinced me to buy an iPad, and now I can't imagine life without it.

Rod and I get to the park at about the same time. On the road, we'll generally either take one of the team buses or sometimes a cab. But once we arrive, we go our separate ways.

As the play-by-play guy, I have different responsibilities. I try to listen to the manager's meeting before batting practice. Sometimes I have specific questions, but other times I just listen to what's on the skipper's mind. After that I make my way into the clubhouse. Again, I might be seeking out specific information or just trying to get the vibe of the team.

Once batting practice starts, I usually head to the announcer booth to go over my notes for the game. Many times, Rod hangs out at the batting cage. He chats with the coaches or just watches the players hit. This is where Rod's playing and coaching background really comes into play. We can both see the same guy hitting, and he'll pick out something technical that I would never see.

We then have dinner with the producer, director, and graphics people. The purpose of these dinners is partly to feed ourselves and partly to flush out different ideas and directions we might go. Once our meeting is over, Rod and I go to the booth, and we're there for the duration.

So as you can see, we're together all the time, but not always together in the same place.

Step Away from the Scorecard!

Baseball players are notoriously sensitive to people touching their stuff. Whether it's a cap, game bats, or even their sunglasses, the unwritten rule is, "Don't ever touch a player's equipment." I won't even get into trying on a player's glove. That is sacrilegious.

Over the years I have formed the same mentality toward my scorecard. I actually can't explain why. Everyone fills out their scorecard differently. Each night, it takes a good hour or so to completely fill out my scorecard. From the lineups to the umpire rotation to stats and biographical information, this simple piece of paper sets the tone for the whole night. Everything has its own spot, and everything must be in the right place.

Here's how I approach my scorecard. You can look, but *do not touch*. I don't have a rational reason for it, but I really believe that if something is amiss, it will affect my broadcast.

Mind you, my sheet is far from neat or perfect, but it's the way I want it. If something disrupts the look or flow of the scorecard, it bothers me for at least a couple innings before I eventually forget about it.

Beauty is in the eyes of the beholder. As score sheets go, Tigers radio man Dan Dickerson has the neatest, most visually appealing sheet I have ever seen. It looks like it was done by a professional calligrapher. Mine is more of a scattered mess, but it works for me. Dan and I often talk about how we become a mess if something is spilled on our scorecards. To tell you the truth, it makes me feel better to know that someone is as nuts as me.

I have had my share of scorecard calamities over the years. Several years ago, the public relations department brought in a family that had won a contest, and the prize was to visit the booth. For someone as regimented as me, something like that can throw me off schedule, but usually it's not a big deal. Everything was going well…until the child dumped a whole sippy cup of juice all over my sheet.

My mind was working like a movie scene. Everything happened in slow motion. I could hear my brain screaming, "NOOOOOOO! Get that kid out of here!"

Of course, I had to play the good sport, so I simply chuckled and drained the grape juice off the card. But I was ruined for the first few innings.

Then there was the time in Chicago when the maintenance guy came into the booth to fix an air conditioning vent in the ceiling. My scorecard was on the counter, just minding its own business. Instead of using a ladder, this guy climbed up and planted his muddy boot smack on top of the middle of my scorecard. As he was taking the first step, I shouted, "No, don't step on my…" But it was too late.

"Relax," he said. "It's only a piece of paper."

Just kill me. If I could have moved the counter and stranded him up in the ceiling, I would have done it.

Sometimes I have only myself to blame. Two seasons ago I was getting ready to broadcast the second game of a doubleheader between the Tigers and Red Sox. It was Verlander versus Beckett, and it was going to be a heavily viewed broadcast. We were already out of our routine because it was a rain make-up game, and originally we were told we weren't going to be able to broadcast it. Thanks to some last minute maneuvering with MLB, however, we were able to show the game.

Ten minutes before airtime, I decided to grab a quick cup of coffee to get through what had been a long day. I placed the coffee on the counter and went to put on my headset. The cord wrapped around the cup and, within a split second, my perfect score sheet was a sloppy brown mess.

Our stage manager, Chuck Fair, had a look of horror on his face. We've worked together long enough that he knows my idiosyncrasies, including my scorecard obsession. He knew we were in trouble. I turned to Chuck and yelled, "Chuckie, I'm screwed! Now what?"

Chuck calmly grabbed the sheet, blotted it dry, and held it for five minutes against a fan to dry it off.

For three innings. Verlander versus Beckett meant little. The only thing that mattered was the warped, brown scorecard I was staring at. Years later, I can't even tell you who won the game, but I can tell you where not to put your coffee.

CHAPTER 6
MAGIC MOMENTS

Maggs' Homer

One of the greatest things about calling games is the possibility of the unknown. This is why I love my job. Whether it's describing a no-hitter (which I've done four times in the majors) or a special milestone, when you get to the ballpark, you never know what might happen.

For many reasons, my favorite moment happened on October 14, 2006. This was the night when the impossible became possible.

I came back to Detroit in 2002. The Tigers proceeded to lose 106 games and finish in last place. The team couldn't get any worse...or so I thought. In 2003, everything went wrong. An American League record 119 losses. Think about that—119 losses. And this was after winning five of their last six games! The Tigers were the butt of a lot of jokes. Trying to keep viewers engaged that season was perhaps the most challenging assignment of my career.

That offseason, general manager Dave Dombrowski started to change the complexion of the team. With the blessing of Mike Ilitch, the Tigers went out and signed All-Star catcher Ivan "Pudge" Rodriguez. Why did Pudge choose Motown? Maybe he saw some potential, or maybe it was about the money. Either way, this was the team's first step towards respectability.

Then in the winter of 2004, Dombrowski rolled the dice. Magglio Ordonez had played in only 52 games, and had undergone major knee surgery. Maggs' injury left him with an uncertain future, but Dombrowski pushed his chips to the middle of the table and signed Ordonez to a six-year contract.

Unfortunately, the Tigers finished with only 71 wins in 2005. While progress had been made, it seemed the postseason was still a bit further down the road.

Then 2006 happened. New manager Jim Leyland set the tone after an early season loss, letting his team know that lackadaisical play would no longer be tolerated. That explosion got the team pointed in the right direction, and five months later, we were in Game 4 of the American League Championship Series, with a chance to go to the World Series.

One of the most dramatic moments in recent Tigers history electrified the city. It was when Magglio hit the game-winning, walk-off homer against Huston Street of the Athletics.

I'm often asked how I felt when I saw the ball leave the park. That's a great question. There's just one problem—I never saw it.

Because the game was on FOX Network as opposed to FOX Sports Detroit, I was part of the "overflow" media that was seated in the right-field bleachers. We wouldn't be able to go on the air until after the game was over. Then we would provide interviews, analysis, and perspective. And by the way, it was 41 degrees out with 15-mph winds.

The game was tied at 3–3 going into the bottom of the eighth inning. At that point, our group decided to head over to the "regular" press box to try to warm up and formulate our game plan.

Magglio Ordonez hits a three run home run in the ninth inning against A's pitcher Huston Street in Game 4 of the ALCS in Detroit on Saturday, October 14, 2006. The Tigers defeated the Athletics 6–3 to sweep the series and advance to the World Series. *(AP Photo/Michael Conroy)*

In the bottom of the ninth, the Tigers started to rally, so postgame host John Keating and his producer decided that they would go straight to the field after the last pitch. Myself and coordinating producer Mike Isenberg headed downstairs outside the clubhouse. Remember, the game was still tied, and we didn't know if we'd be waiting 20 minutes or two hours.

A group of reporters were glued to the television just outside the Tigers clubhouse. The second Maggs made contact, I remember thinking that I had to get to the field as quickly as possible. I didn't even see the ball leave the yard on television.

Because the clubhouse wasn't open yet, we had to run up to the main concourse. The ballpark was in a frenzy. I had to fight my way through the crowd and jump over the railing to get to the field while at the same time high-fiving fans and pinballing through a mass of ecstatic humanity.

The whole experience was the most electric moment of my career. Just thinking about it gives me goose bumps. To realize where this team had come from, literally as low as you can go, to the World Series in a span of three years, and combined with the energy from the fans—well, it was a night I'll never forget.

Even now, six years later, I watch the game over and over on my DVR. I have to since I never saw the homer live.

The Kid

One of the great illusions of television is that it makes the game of baseball appear easy. Amazing feats like throwing a baseball 100 mph and then turning on that same pitch and hitting it out are minimized by the great skills possessed by major league players. And as hard as we try, it's really impossible to show how difficult these tasks are.

Of course, some moments scream, "Incredible!" but others are more subtle. And the truly great players make the impossible seem simple.

I've seen a lot of Hall of Fame players during my career—Barry Bonds, Greg Maddux, Cal Ripken, and the list goes on. But there are few players who have left me in awe more than Ken Griffey Jr.

Scouts talk about five tool players, and this is what they're talking about.

Speed? Check.

Defensive ability? Big check.

Arm strength? Check.

Hit for average? Check.

Hit for power? Check plus, plus, plus.

This guy was already great when he was 19 years old.

One of the greatest unknowns in baseball history is what Griffey's numbers would have been had he not battled injuries throughout his entire career.

My favorite part of interleague play is that it gives fans a chance to see baseball's best players from the other league. Because Griffey spent the first 11 seasons of his career in Seattle, he was no stranger to Tigers fans. In 2000, he departed to play for his hometown Cincinnati Reds. "The Kid" was on the back nine of his career, but he was still a dangerous hitter. In 2006, he hit 27 home runs in just 109 games.

This was May 2006, and the Tigers were rolling to the AL pennant and had opened up a 5–1 lead on the Reds in a May matchup at Comerica Park. This had the appearance of just another one of 162 games. In the seventh inning, Adam Dunn led off with a home run for the Reds. Then they loaded the bases. Tigers skipper Jim Leyland had seen enough.

Few rookies, let alone middle relievers, have ever had the impact that Joel Zumaya had that season. For him, 100-mph fastballs were commonplace, and he may have been the most un-hittable pitcher in baseball that season.

Zoom rolled in from the bullpen to face Junior Griffey. This had all the makings of a classic matchup.

The count went to 1–1. Zumaya was not leaving anything to chance. He reared back and fired a pitch that registered 103 mph. Actually, it came in at 103 mph, but it left at about twice that speed.

With a simple flick of the wrist, Griffey unloaded a grand slam, giving the Reds the lead.

The Tigers would win the game on a Cincinnati error in the bottom of the tenth inning, but that was almost irrelevant. Watching a 36-year-old man turn around a 103-mph fastball was absolutely stunning.

That May evening confirmed what I had already thought. Ken Griffey Jr. was the best all-around player I've ever seen in person, and I was truly blessed to have the best seat in the house.

All Night Long

As I've already mentioned, one of the great things about baseball is that you never know when you're going to experience something you'll never forget. On August 24, 2007, I experienced the perfect storm—literally.

The Tigers were starting a four-game series with the New York Yankees at Comerica Park. Anytime the big, bad Yankees come to town, it's a big deal, and since 1996, it's been even more special with Kalamazoo, Michigan, native Derek Jeter on the Yankees' roster. On this night, an aging Roger Clemens was to take the mound, so there was some extra buzz at the park.

On top of that, we were going to have a new broadcast team because my regular partner, Rod Allen, was sidelined with a bad back. We were fortunate to be able to grab former Tigers pitcher Dan Petry on short notice. Little did the former All-Star know what was on deck.

Dan had a business meeting the next morning and was hoping for a quick game. In the back of my mind, I was already skeptical of that because Yankees games always take forever. The batters work the count, take a ton of pitches, and the Yanks and the Red Sox are two teams when it's best to clear out the night to watch them play.

At about 5:00 PM, the Michigan skies literally opened up. The storm was so heavy that I practically expected to see an ark coming out of right field.

By game time at 7:00 PM, we couldn't even see the floor of the Tigers dugout. John Keating, our pregame host, finished his show and went to join his family in Grand Haven. He called to tell us that Interstate 75, a major highway, was closed due to flooding.

When it comes to weather, the thinking in baseball has changed over the years. When I was growing up, doubleheaders were commonplace, so if there was a rainout, playing two games the next day was not a big deal.

Particularly in the 2000s, doubleheaders have become a dirty word. They are almost never scheduled, and when the teams do play two, it's almost always a day/night affair. Teams like to have a break before burning out their pitching staffs, and they also like to have separate admissions.

With the Yankees making their only Detroit appearance of the season, the umpires felt pressure to get this game in. All teams have sophisticated equipment and radar to figure out when there will be a window to play, and the Tigers staff was convinced we'd get this one in.

But 7:00 PM became 8:00, then 8:00 PM became 9:00. Still, the officials were confident we'd get this one in.

We were basically shooting the breeze in the booth. During a long rain delay, the channel will typically go to "fill" programming, such as a *Tigers Weekly* episode or something along those lines. We will come on every half hour or so, just to give people an update on the situation.

At about 10:15, we got word that yes, there would be baseball. The first pitch would be thrown at about 11:05 PM.

"Seriously? We're gonna start this thing?" I asked stage manager Chuck Fair.

"Afraid so," Chuck answered.

If announcers are truthful about delays, they will tell you it is really difficult to get your energy level back up after a delay. One-hour delays are bad enough, but we had been sitting for four hours.

"Chuckie, get me some toothpicks because I'm gonna need something to prop my eyes open before this one is over," I said.

By the time we got started, there was still rain, but it was off and on. Magglio Ordonez got the Tigers off to a good start with a two-run homer off of Clemens in the first inning.

The lead would eventually grow to 6–3, but as anyone who watches the Yankees knows, they never seem to go away. In the fifth inning, catcher Jorge Posada belted a two-run double against Andrew Miller. Then designated hitter Hideki Matsui tied the game with an RBI single.

It was already past midnight, and Dan and I didn't have to say a word. We were both getting the same feeling that this was going to go on for awhile.

The next thing we knew, it was 2:00 AM and we were heading for extra innings.

The tenth came and went, and soon the Tigers were up with two outs in the bottom of the eleventh. By this point, I had resigned myself to the fact that this game was never going to end, and I would just live in our booth until the next game.

But then there was a flicker of life. Sean Casey singled, then Magglio did the same. Two men on, but two out. Carlos Guillen was up.

As the clock struck 3:30, Guillen became my favorite player ever when he ripped a three-run homer off reliever Sean Henn, and the 4-hour, 24-minute marathon was finally over.

The hearty Tigers fans who had stuck around danced while Lionel Ritchie's "All Night Long" blared on the loud speakers. I never got a chance to ask Dan Petry how his early-morning meeting went. Let's just say I'm sure it was quicker than the game.

2,131

When a team's season schedule comes out, just about everyone takes a quick look. Who do they open the season against? When are the games against our hated rivals? When do they make trips to certain cities? It doesn't matter how long you've been around the game, whether you're the manager or a player, this almost always happens.

My first season broadcasting baseball in the major leagues was 1995. After eight long seasons in the minors, I had finally got my first shot in the big leagues with the California Angels.

If you've seen the Steve Martin movie, *The Jerk*, you surely remember when the new phone book comes out and Navin Johnson celebrates that he's in it. "I am somebody!" he shouts. This was similar to how I felt when the Angels put out their schedule.

There were specific games I wanted to find. When were we going to New York? What about Boston? But of course, the biggest question I had was when we would be coming to Detroit. Getting to broadcast games in Yankee Stadium and Fenway Park would be moments to treasure, but for me, nothing could really compare to Tiger Stadium.

To be able to sit in the booth near Ernie Harwell, in the stadium where I went countless times as a kid…well, let's just say it was going to be a dream come true.

Three other dates caught my eye as well. On September 4, 5, and 6, the Angels would be in Baltimore. On the surface, this was no big deal. The Orioles were a pretty forgettable team that season. (They would finish with a 71–73 record.) But as I counted the days toward one of baseball's biggest events that year, it dawned on me that we were going to be at Camden Yards for one of the all-time greatest moments in baseball history.

We've all heard the saying that records are made to be broken, and for the most part they are. Hank Aaron's home-run mark was passed by Barry Bonds (with a little help). Rickey Henderson shattered Lou Brock's steals record. And one day, someone will probably surpass Joe Dimaggio's 56-game hitting streak.

But nobody was supposed to pass the unbreakable record—Lou Gehrig's 2,130 consecutive games. I mean, it took a fatal disease to get him out of the lineup. That's a pretty remarkable record.

Sure enough, as I did the math, Cal Ripken was on pace to break the Iron Horse's record, and if everything fell right, it would happen on September 6 against the Angels.

My first season in the bigs was definitely one to remember. The Angels had taken control of the American League West early on and were cruising to a division title. By August 9, we had an 11-game lead. Then things changed.

As the team entered September, their lead was down to 7½ games. You'd normally feel good going into the last month of the season with that kind of lead, but the Angels were letting it slip away.

On the way to Baltimore, I had two distinctly different emotions. First, of course, was dealing with the day-to-day collapse of the team I was covering. But the other was really incredible—I was going to witness Ripken breaking one of the most amazing records in all of sports.

We flew into Baltimore on the evening of September 3, fresh off the Boston Red Sox lighting up our ace, Chuck Finley, in an 8–1 demolition.

Of course, everyone knew what was going on with Cal. He was now just two games away from tying the record and three away from breaking it. This week would have a playoff atmosphere, with the Angels trying to hold on, but more significantly, the eyes of an entire nation were on Ripken's coronation as the ultimate iron man.

The three-game series began on a Monday, and the Angels spoiled the party that day by beating the Orioles behind Jim Abbott 5–3. Even in defeat, Cal provided a harbinger of things to come, hitting a home run in his 2,129th consecutive game. Talk about rising to the occasion. Ripken was in the beginning of the autumn of his career. In 1995, he would finish with only 17 home runs, batting just .262. But he always knew how to seize the moment, and this week was the moment of all moments.

The next night, Ripken would equal Gehrig's mark in game 2,130 and, as the storybook event unfolded, Cal hit a sixth-inning home run off Angels reliever Mark Holzemer. I was at the mic in the middle innings, so I got to call Ripken's home run on the night he tied Gehrig. I can still see the ball flying over the left-field wall. The homer gave the Orioles an 8–0 lead, and I had to force myself into toning down the call so as not to seem too excited about yet another inevitable Angels loss. The Orioles would win the game 8–0, and the Angels lead in the west plummeted to 5½ games. Cal was now tied with Lou Gehrig.

On Wednesday, September 6, I arrived at Camden Yards early along with producer Kirt Daniels. Fans were already gathered around the park at 3:30, and Eutaw street was abuzz. I've since attended playoff and World Series games, but I've never experienced anything like that. President Clinton would be on hand, and Secret Service members had the press box on lock down.

Kirt and I decided that my partner, Bob Starr, would call the fifth inning when Cal officially broke the record. Bob was a mentor to me, and I had great respect for his ability and experience. It was only right that he called the record even though I typically called the fourth, fifth, and sixth innings.

With Bob at the mic, the Angels went 1-2-3 against Mike Mussina in the top of the fifth, and the game became official. Ripken had broken a record that many people thought would never even be approached—2,131 straight games without taking a day off. Bob did a masterful job of describing the scene as Ripken took a tour around the warning track, shaking hands and high-fiving fans.

President Clinton was in the television booth next to me, and I was nearly overwhelmed by the event. As Bob continued to describe the history-making accomplishment, I just sat there with my mic turned off. Finally, Bob killed his mic and looked at me.

"Well, young man, aren't you going to say anything?" he asked.

I just grinned at him and said, "Nope. This is your show." The truth is, I didn't want to say something stupid and screw up the moment.

The moment was truly overwhelming, even to the Angels. In the midst of one of baseball's greatest collapses, the team stood at the top step of the dugout and gave Ripken a standing ovation. The fans were on their feet for 22 minutes.

Then, as if choreographed, Cal did a lap around the stadium at the urging of teammates Bobby Bonilla and Rafael Palmeiro. He initially resisted, but he finally gave in.

And like any Hollywood movie, Ripken would homer for the third consecutive game. Again, even the Angels couldn't be too mad at what was happening. This night was bigger than the Orioles and bigger than the Angels' collapse. This was baseball history, and once again I had the best seat in the house.

As the game moved to the later innings, I used a between-innings break to head to the bathroom. As I opened the door to leave the booth, I was immediately stopped by the Secret Service.

"Sir, I'll need you to stay in the booth," an agent told me as he held out his arm.

"Why?"

"You can't leave until the president has left the press box."

"But I have to go to the bathroom," I said.

"You'll have to hold it."

"Well, how many more innings is he going to stay?"

"I can't answer that."

So there I sat, staring at the President of the United States trough the glass window that separated our booths for another inning, praying he would decide to call it a night. The fact that I was that close to the president should have been a thrill. But my bladder wasn't impressed.

I feel pretty safe in saying that nobody will ever play in 2,632 consecutive games like Cal Ripken did. I mean, just look at the math. Ripken's streak is 502 games longer than Lou Gehrig's. That's more than three full seasons, and it's more than double the third-longest streak of Everett Scott.

Not that I'd ever forget September 6, 1995, but I do have a photo taken on the field with the B&O warehouse in the backdrop draped with the 2,131 banner and a tape of the game. The next season, when the Orioles visited Anaheim, Ripken signed my score sheet from the record-breaking night.

Greatness Meets Greatness

There are some moments in baseball that will stay with you forever. The classic confrontations etch themselves in your memory. Think about Reggie Jackson versus Bob Welch in the Yankees-Dodgers World Series, or Kirk Gibson's dramatic home run against Dennis Eckersley in 1988. These, of course, were postseason moments.

But once in a while, a regular-season matchup lives up to the billing. In August 2013, I was fortunate enough to have a front-row seat for a clash between two future Hall of Famers.

The Tigers came to Yankee Stadium with the look of a team ready to run away with the Central Division title. They had just swept second-place Cleveland and now led the Indians by seven games. The Yankees were 11 games out of first place, but a trip to New York always feels like the playoffs.

Across the field, there was a much different vibe. The once-powerful Yankees spent the entire season being overwhelmed by injuries. Derek Jeter had been out most of the year with leg problems stemming from the previous year's ALDS against the Tigers. Mark Teixeira needed surgery on his wrist, ending his year after just 15 games. Former Tiger Curtis Granderson broke his hand in his first spring training game of the season, then he came back and broke his pinkie. Starting third baseman Kevin Youkilis had back surgery, and catcher Francisco Cervelli broke his hand.

But it was more than just injuries. Starter CC Sabathia was showing his age, while Hiroki Kuroda and Andy Pettitte were seemingly on the verge of retirement. And of course, there was Alex Rodriguez, who had just returned from hip surgery—and was facing a 211-game suspension (later reduced to 162 games) from a steroid scandal.

The series opener didn't seem like anything special. Rick Porcello took the hill for Detroit against Ivan Nova. Porcello pitched decently, giving up three runs in five innings, while the tall, right-handed Nova was superb, allowing just a single run through seven. It wasn't totally surprising that the Tigers to come out a bit flat. The Cleveland series was billed as a huge showdown, so a letdown was almost to be expected.

New York held a 3–1 lead going into the ninth inning. For the past 18 years, that has meant one thing to Yankees fans—"Enter Sandman" blasts over the speakers for the greatest closer of all time, Mariano Rivera.

It had been quite a summer for Mo. In spring training, he announced that 2013 would be his last season. Coming back from the previous year's torn ACL, Rivera looked as good as ever. He had 35 saves in 38 chances, with an ERA of 1.70. In July's All-Star Game, he was the main story, entering the game in the eighth inning and receiving a standing ovation—from both teams. Being named the game's MVP was merely a formality.

Don Kelly led off for Detroit by flying out to center field. Then it was back to the top of the order, and Austin Jackson ripped a double to left center.

Hmm, I thought, *Even as dominant as Mariano has been, he doesn't always go 1-2-3.*

Then Torii Hunter grounded out back to the mound. That set up a showdown between the most dominant reliever ever against the best hitter I've ever seen—Mariano Rivera versus Miguel Cabrera. Cabrera was playing at less than 100 percent, battling leg and abdominal injuries. Still, you could feel the buzz in the stadium as Miggy ambled to the plate.

Tigers fans had seen Cabrera come through in the clutch time after time. In fact, he hit a huge eighth-inning home run in Cleveland just days before. But this was Mariano Rivera.

Cabrera worked the count to 2–2, but not without some pain. He fouled one pitch off his sore leg, then another one off his knee. Throw in the strained midsection, and this looked like it was going to be a Yankees victory.

Yankees relief pitcher Mariano Rivera delivers in the ninth-inning against the Detroit Tigers on Sunday, August 11, 2013, in New York. Although Rivera blew a save allowing consecutive game home runs to Tigers' Miguel Cabrera and another to designated hitter Victor Martinez, he still earned a win when the Yankees' Brett Gardner hit a walk-off, solo home run in the bottom of the ninth and the Yankees won 5–4. *(AP Photo/Kathy Willens)*

As Cabrera hobbled back into the batter's box, I remember thinking that would just make this all the more dramatic. For some reason, I truly believed he could hit one out. Given the circumstances, maybe I was thinking more with my heart than my head.

Miguel grimaced as he stepped back in the box, and then it happened.

Cabrera launched a 2–2 pitch over the center-field wall, and as the ball sailed over the boards, our cameras picked up Rivera mouthing the word, "Wow!"

In the blink of an eye, the Tigers had tied the game in the ninth against the greatest save artist of all time. I don't usually leave me seat, but on this occasion I jumped out of my chair with my hands raised and screamed the game-tying call. My style has always been one of controlled excitement, but this time I lost it. I looked over to Rod, and we were both stunned by what had just happened.

I have never covered a player who has such a flair for the dramatic like Miggy. A lot of guys can hit home runs in the big leagues but it is the player who can hit one when his club needs it the most that makes him special.

As Cabrera rounded third, it seemed as if Yankees fans didn't know whether to boo or bow. It almost didn't matter that the Tigers lost in 10 on a Brett Gardner single because Miggy had slain the king.

This felt like a once-in-a-lifetime experience...until it happened again two days later.

This time the Yankees led 4–2 heading into the ninth. The speakers blasted "Enter Sandman," and Mariano Rivera came into the exact same setup, except this time, Cabrera led things off.

Again, the count went to 2–2. And again, Miggy took Rivera deep for another home run. Where Mariano was almost bemused by the first shot, you could tell he was really mad about this one. It was the first time in the great career of Rivera that he had given up consecutive home runs to the same batter. The only problem for the Tigers was that the score was still 4–3.

Prince Fielder lined out to third, then it was Victor Martinez's turn. V-Mart crushed Rivera's 0–1 pitch into the right-field seats, and the game was tied. Suffice it to say the greatest closer of all time never had a weekend like that.

Incredibly, the Tigers lost again when Brett Gardner (again) delivered the game-winning shot, this time with a home run off of Jose Veras.

The fact remains that Mariano is still the greatest closer in the history of the game. But for one August weekend, he was just another notch on Miguel Cabrera's belt.

———

People often ask me what has been my greatest thrill was broadcasting. I'm truly blessed to have to struggle with the answer. Justin Verlander's two no-hitters? Armando Galarraga's "imperfect" game? Cal Ripken passing Lou Gehrig for consecutive games played?

The funny thing is that with all of those great moments, perhaps my best memory is actually something I have no memory of.

Confusing? You bet. But let me explain.

Late in the 2013 season, I received a text from my son, Brett. It was right after that incredible weekend Miguel Cabrera had against Mariano Rivera. As I mentioned, it was a two-game stretch the likes of which no one had ever seen.

Brett was checking out some old YouTube videos of Rivera's greatest moments. He was specifically drawn to Mo's first MLB save. My son noticed that it was against the Angels in 1996.

"You broadcasted for the Angels in 1996, right?" the text read.

"Yeah, why?" I replied.

"I'm watching some old videos, and Mariano Rivera saved his first game against the Angels. You were at the mic for his first major league save."

So I decided to check baseballreference.com and, sure enough, Rivera's first major league save was against the Angels.

What most people don't remember about Rivera is that in his rookie year of 1995, he actually made 10 starts. By 1996, he was a critical piece of the Yankees' championship bullpen, working as the setup man for John Wetteland.

On May 17, 1996, at Yankee Stadium, Joe Torre gave this relatively unknown reliever a chance. Rivera entered an 8–5 game in the ninth inning and struck out Randy Velarde. Rivera gave up a single to Mike Aldrete and then got Garret Anderson to bounce into a game-ending double play.

And there it was, the first save in the (soon-to-be Hall of Fame) career of Mariano Rivera. And I was at the mic, broadcasting with my partner, Bob Starr.

Rivera was anything but a household name at the time, so it seemed like just another boring save. If only I had known what was to become of this second-year no-name. The storybook ending would have been that I recognized greatness that day and knew No. 42 would go on to the Hall of Fame. That would make me sound really smart. Alas, I had no idea of what was to come. I look at it this way—if the Yankees knew how great Rivera would turn out to be, they would never have made him a starting pitcher, right?

The truth is, if I hadn't gotten that text, I might not have realized I was there for his first major league save.

The Triple Crown

The 2012 season was one that Tigers fans will never forget. The team swept the hated New York Yankees out of the playoffs and made it to the World Series for just the third time in 28 years. But there's no question that 2012 will always be known as The Year of Miggy.

Nobody since Red Sox Hall of Famer Carl Yastrzemski in 1967 had won baseball's Triple Crown. A few guys made a run at it, but nobody had really come that close—until Miguel Cabrera.

Looking back, maybe we should have seen it coming. Cabrera was one of the few players in the last 40 years to have a *career* Triple Crown, leading the AL in home runs in 2008, RBI in 2010, and batting average the next season. Impressive, yes, but doing it all in the same year, well that would be historic.

Miggy is the most talented hitter I've ever seen—a rare combination of power and average—and he does it seemingly always under control, never changing his mechanics. He's the only guy in baseball who actually surprises me when he makes an out.

Tigers fans had already been spoiled the previous year with Justin Verlander's MVP/Cy Young Award double dip, when he won pitching's Triple Crown. But to do what Cabrera was attempting with a bat hadn't been achieved in 35 years.

Miggy's season was characterized by consistent dominance—the guy never went into a slump. But even with that, things were still unsettled going into the Tigers' final series in Kansas City. The Royals had nothing to play for—they finished 16 games out of first place and 18 games under .500. But for everyone who loves the Tigers, all eyes were on Kansas City.

Heading into the last game, Cabrera was in pretty good shape. He led Josh Hamilton by 11 RBI, so that category was wrapped up. In the race for batting championship, Miggy was at .331, a nearly insurmountable lead over Mike Trout's .324. The home-run chase was still up in the air—his 44 long balls led Hamilton by one and Curtis Granderson by three.

Jim Leyland was getting updates in the dugout, and soon it became official that Miguel had wrapped up the batting title. Trout capped off a remarkable rookie season by going 2–3. He'd finish the year at .326. Great, but not great enough.

The only drama left was to see if Hamilton could go deep twice or Granderson thrice. If there was to be a tie for homers, Cabrera would get credit for the Triple Crown. (In 1967, Yastrzemski and Harmon Killebrew both hit 44 home runs.)

Hamilton ended up going 1–5 without any home runs, so the former MVP finished with 43. Things were a little more interesting in the Bronx.

The Yankees crushed Boston 14–2, and Granderson was having a day. Cabrera's former teammate went yard twice in the first seven innings and may have gotten one more chance. Anyone who knows Curtis will tell you what a class act he is on and off the field. He knew the home run scenario—the Yankees game started an hour before the Tigers took the field—yet he pulled himself after homering in the seventh, ensuring Cabrera won the title.

Once Leyland received the update, he choreographed a moment I'll never forget. Team president David Dombrowski was in the broadcast booth with us, and he pointed out in the bottom of the fourth inning that Cabrera was coming out of the game. With the Triple Crown in tow, the team wanted to give Miggy the rest of the night off and a proper exit.

Now remember, we were in Kansas City—it was the meaningless last game of a meaningless season for the Royals. But the baseball fans in the Show Me state have always been astute, and on this night, they once again showed their appreciation for the game. They gave Miggy a standing ovation—the guy who had crushed their team time and time again. After a curtain call, baseball's newest Triple Crown champion came back into the dugout and embraced his manager. Neither man would ever forget what the other had done for him.

But it was the manager in the other dugout, Royals skipper Ned Yost, who put it succinctly and accurately, "I don't know if I've ever seen anything like it. It ranks up there with a 30-win season, with hitting .400. It's extremely tough to do. I don't know if we'll ever see it again."

I agree.

CHAPTER 7
NO-HITTERS

Must See JV

Really, Justin Verlander shouldn't have been a Detroit Tiger.

By virtue of a 64–98 record the previous year, the San Diego Padres owned the first pick in the 2004 draft. As usual, every team was looking for the same thing—eight of the first ten picks were pitchers.

But also as usual, the Padres were watching their payroll. So instead of taking a more expensive pitcher, the Padres drafted high school shortstop Matt Bush. Bush would end up in trouble with the law, eventually ending up behind bars. That left such arms as Verlander and Jered Weaver available at the second spot.

One thing you can say about the Tigers—they aren't afraid to spend on quality. General manager Dave Dombrowski knows that owner Mike Ilitch wants to win. And in baseball, you have to spend to win, especially on your minor league system.

Once the Padres took Bush, Detroit pounced on Verlander. They knew that between his incredible talent and his four years of college experience, JV would be on the fast track to the bigs. It didn't even take a full year before Justin was making his major league debut.

Make no mistake about it—there was already a buzz for the 22-year-old righty. In 20 minor league starts, JV was 11–2 with an incredible 1.29 ERA. In 118-plus innings, he struck out 136 batters.

On July 4, 2005, the Tigers got to unwrap their new toy. But on face value, Verlander's debut was nothing to write home about. In 5⅓ innings, Verlander accumulated four runs on seven hits, with four strikeouts and three walks. In his first inning, Justin gave up three consecutive hits, including two by future teammates Victor Martinez and Jhonny Peralta. The Indians jumped out to a 3–0 lead.

The rookie settled in after that. Travis Hafner became Justin's first major league strikeout, but the most valuable lesson Verlander learned was that he couldn't just throw it by big leaguers. As gifted as Justin has always been, perhaps his biggest asset is between his ears.

After one more mediocre start, Justin went back to the minors, determined to stick for good the next time.

Justin Verlander throws against the Houston Astros during a game in Detroit on June 28, 2006. Verlander easily won the AL Rookie of the Year honor, as he was listed first on 26-of-28 ballots for a total of 133 points. *(AP Photo/Paul Sancya)*

In 2006, everything started to come together. the Tigers got their first Rookie of the Year since 1978 as well as their Game 1 starter for the World Series.

———

The two defining moments for Justin were performances that Tigers fans will never forget—and neither will the opposing hitters, for that matter.

In June 2007, the Tigers hosted Milwaukee in what seemed to be just another game on the schedule. Both teams would end up finishing second in their divisions, but as fans learned, any time Justin Verlander takes the mound, it's an event, not just a game.

You might say this game was for the birds. A flock of seagulls swarmed around the field all night. As it turned out, the birds might have had a better chance to get a hit than the Brewers.

JV came out smoking, striking out the first two Milwaukee hitters. In the fourth, he whiffed the side. The only chance the Brew Crew had this night was getting a base on balls since Verlander did walk four batters.

The Tigers defense did its part, too. Neifi Perez turned a beautiful 6–4–3 double play to end the eighth inning. That was about all the help Justin needed. By the top of the ninth, he had thrown only 101 pitches. JV was just getting warmed up.

Up stepped Craig Counsell. Four pitches later and he was sitting down, becoming strikeout victim No. 11. Three more pitches and Tony Graffanino was sitting beside Counsell as strikeout No. 12.

Before the last hitter (J.J. Hardy), Justin walked around the mound in an attempt to relax. He was now on the verge of history. In came a fastball at 101 mph. I got the feeling that Verlander wasn't getting tired. I remember thinking, *It's the ninth inning, and this guy is throwing 101 mph. Who does that on this planet?*

Then Hardy swung late at a pitch and hit a fly ball to right field. Magglio Ordonez pulled it in, and Comerica Park had its first no-hitter.

————

What happened May 7, 2011, in Toronto may have been the difference between a good year and one for the ages.

During spring training, Verlander made a conscious effort to bring intensity to each appearance, hoping this would help him get off to a good start in the regular season. Traditionally, April had not been a strong month for JV.

When the Tigers took on the Blue Jays, Verlander was only 2–3 but had actually pitched well.

Like the Brewers nearly four years earlier, the Blue Jays didn't have a chance. Justin used a slightly different game plan for this one. Yes, he was still throwing gas, but this time the defense was much more involved. The first seven innings were perfect, even with just three strikeouts.

In the eighth, J.P. Arencibia worked a walk to spoil the perfect game. The Jays excitement was short-lived, however, when Edwin Encarnacion hit into a 6-4-3 double play. Verlander was now just three outs away from another no-hitter.

In the bottom of the ninth, Justin faced the 7-8-9 hitters. David Cooper popped to second for the first out. Then John McDonald bounced out to second.

The last hitter, Rajai Davis, could have stepped up to the plate with a two-by-four and it would not have made a difference. Verlander struck him out, and history was his for a second time.

You've got to give Blue Jay fans credit—they knew what they had seen, and they gave Verlander a standing ovation.

As excited as I was in the booth, it was stunning to see the matter-of-fact reaction of Verlander. His wry smile seemed to indicate that he knew the Jays had no chance. Justin truly believes he will throw a no-hitter every start, and at this point, I think so, too. He came within two outs of his third no-no in 2012 before the Pirates Josh Harrison singled with one out in the ninth. In 2013 Verlander also brought no-hit bids into the seventh inning against the Rangers and Astros.

I don't think major league players are often intimidated by a pitcher, but in JV's Cy Young Award and MVP season of 2011, I'll bet a few never complained about a night off with Verlander on the hill.

28 Up, 28 Down

As I've said, one of the things I love most about my job is that you never know when something special is going to happen. What makes it even more strange is that you have no control over it, either.

I've been fortunate to call five no-hitters during my career. (Thanks, Justin Verlander!) But I've never been behind the mic for a perfect game. There have only been 20 perfectos in baseball history, but like a fan waiting to catch a foul ball, I keep hoping.

And June 2, 2010, seemed like the most unlikely night to accomplish a lifelong goal. It was 70 degrees with two good but mostly average major league pitchers, Armando Galarraga and Fausto Carmona, facing off against each other. Little did any of us know that this would be a night that would live on in baseball history forever.

Galarraga, a journeyman right hander who had some moderate big-league success leading up to this start, was 20–18 lifetime.

Armando was capable of pitching a good game, and on this night, he retired the first nine Indians—five on ground balls. He seemed to be exerting so little effort that I don't even know if he worked up a sweat.

Oakland's Dallas Braden and Roy Halladay of the Phillies had already thrown perfect games in May, and as we got to the middle innings, I began to wonder, "Could it happen again?"

As a broadcaster you have to fight the urge to get too excited about the potential of a no hitter or perfect game. Lots of guys throw no-hitters for three innings. For me, the rule of thumb is I never get excited until I see 18 up and 18 down, or six innings of no-hit ball. That is the point in a game when I believe a pitcher has a legitimate shot at throwing a no-hitter or perfect game.

As Galarraga took the mound in the sixth inning, he had already retired 15 straight Indians. Now one of the traditions in baseball is that when a pitcher has a no-no going, his teammates don't talk to him. Heck, they don't even sit near him. On TV, my partner, Rod Allen, and I won't mention it, either. On the radio it's different because fans have no other way of knowing what's going on. With us, viewers can see the graphics, so we follow the superstition.

The sixth inning went according to plan. Mark Grudzielanek struck out swinging to start the inning. Sixteen straight. Then Mike Redmond flied to Austin Jackson in centerfield. Seventeen straight. Jason Donald lined out to Magglio Ordonez in right. Eighteen straight.

Now it was on. Not only was a no hitter in sight, but so was a perfect game. Two more groundouts in a 1-2-3 seventh inning, and Galarraga had the crowd of just less than 18,000 believing that they were witnessing something special.

As we approached the top of the eighth, the Tigers led 1–0. This is a potential nightmare scenario for any manager. He's juggling a perfect game with making sure you win the game. Baseball is littered with situations just like this, where the manager has to make the call. Does he take out the pitcher and risk the game? Or does he give his pitcher a chance at history?

Galarraga, meanwhile, was making his manager Jim Leyland's job easy. The eighth inning was nice and quick. Travis Hafner grounded to short for the first out. Jhonny Peralta struck out swinging for the second out. And when Russell Branyan grounded out to Carlos Guillen at second base, Galarraga was just three outs away from a perfect game.

With the crowd roaring, Galarraga and Leyland's night became a much simpler proposition. Magglio Ordonez ripped a two-run single, and the Tigers led 3–0. The win was relatively secure, so now it was Armando's chance at history.

Well-traveled infielder Mark Grudzielanek would lead off the ninth for the Indians. Twenty-four Indians had come to bat, and 24 frustrated Indians went back to the dugout. Galarraga was just three outs away from history.

Just about every no-hitter has one outstanding defensive play that keeps things going—a great catch or a tremendous throw that lives on forever. To this point, Armando had been too good. There were really no close calls while he dominated the Cleveland lineup. That was about to change.

Grudzielanek drove a Galarraga offering deep into the left-center sky. This thing had double written all over it. For a split second, I knew my chance at calling a perfect game was history. But somehow, rookie Austin Jackson, in a dead sprint from center, made one of the biggest and best catches I have ever seen.

With one out, Mike Redmond hit a ground ball to Ramón Santiago at short. The slick-fielding utilityman played it flawlessly for the second out.

Now with the crowd to its feet, Cleveland shortstop Jason Donald strolled to the plate representing the Iandians' last chance.

The nerves kicked in. I kept telling myself, *Don't get fancy, Just call the play.*

These are the moments announcers live for. Their words will be played over and over. I just didn't want to screw it up. I just had to call the play.

With the count 1–1, Donald hit a ground ball to the far right of first baseman Miguel Cabrera. Cabrera vacated his spot, fielded the ball, and tossed it to Galarraga who was covering. Galarraga's foot hit the bag a split second before Donald's.

"Out!" I shouted. "No, he called him safe!"

I knew my mind wasn't playing tricks on me. I had seen this play a thousand times in my career. The pitcher's foot clearly hit the bag before the runner's. But first-base umpire Jim Joyce called him safe. The perfect game was gone. For a split second I doubted what I thought I had seen. Maybe he was safe and I had blown the call.

Our production crew quickly cued up the replay, and it confirmed that Donald was out. Joyce had missed the call, and an entire stadium was livid. Trevor Crowe would eventually ground out to end the game, but the perfect game and the no-hitter were gone.

The human instinct is to pile on the umpire and let him have it for missing such a big call. Oddly, I wasn't angry at Joyce. I just felt bad for him, Galarraga, and the fans who were cheated out of witnessing a perfect game.

It was more a sense of disbelief and disappointment. Joyce realized he made a bad call, and there is nothing we could do to change it.

In the ensuing hours, Joyce was reduced to tears after watching replays of the blown call. He felt so bad that he requested a meeting with Galarraga to apologize. Galarraga's reaction to the incident was somewhat stunning. There was no screaming, no cursing, and no blood boiling over. There was just a painful smile.

Joyce spent the longest night of his life on June 2. He drove to Toledo where he had family and spent the night. The next day, he had to call balls and strikes behind the plate.

Some of the crowd booed Joyce as he took the field that afternoon. But when Armando brought out the lineup card and patted the umpire on the shoulder, much of the pain was gone. The crowd reacted with a standing ovation. Galarraga stood much taller than if he had gotten the perfect game.

That act of kindness and humility is something I'll never forget. While the record book shows a one-hitter for Galarraga that day, my score sheet still says perfect game.

A No-Hitter Like No Other

I have been fortunate to call four no-hitters in my career—two by Justin Verlander, one by Matt Garza, and one by Eric Milton. There have been several close calls—Verlander in 2012 and Anibal Sanchez in 2013 both lost no-hitters in the ninth inning, and of course there was Armando Galarraga's "imperfect" game—but I always figured No. 5 would be another Verlander special.

One of the great things about baseball is that you never know when something special is going to happen, and when you think you know…well, you don't. Having said that, the last day of the 2013 regular season, it seemed like a no-hitter might be possible. The Tigers were in Miami to take on a Marlins team that had already lost 100 games. Justin Verlander was taking the mound, likely trying to make his case to start the playoff opener later in the week. There was no pressure—it was just two teams playing out the string. JV could just blow away the last-place team, right?

With the postseason coming, Jim Leyland decided to rest several of his regulars. An ailing Miguel Cabrera, older veterans Victor Martinez and Torii Hunter, plus Austin Jackson were all out of the lineup.

Starting for the Marlins was Henderson Alvarez, who was acquired in a blockbuster deal from Toronto in the off-season, including All-Stars Jose Reyes and Mark Buehrle. The 23-year-old right-hander was still trying to establish himself as a big leaguer, even though he led the Blue Jays in innings the previous season.

When Marlins owner Jeffrey Loria decides to stop giving away all of his players, Miami could have a very nice pitching staff, thanks to star rookie Jose Fernandez and promising pitchers Nathan Eovaldi and Alvarez. Nobody in south Florida is quite sure when that will be, however.

On this day, Alvarez was throwing well but not overpowering; he didn't record his first strikeout until the sixth inning. Yet none of the Tigers seemed to be able to square up the balls. Their best chance came in the third when Ramon Santiago hit a slicing line drive over the head of Marlins shortstop Adeiny Hechavarria. Somehow, Hechavarria jumped up and snagged it. Something was definitely going on.

In the meantime, Verlander was doing his part with six shutout innings and 10 strikeouts. Doug Fister and Rick Porcello each threw a scoreless inning.

From the Tigers standpoint, this playoff tune-up felt more like a spring training game. Alvarez was cruising along, and the next thing I knew, we were in the ninth inning and he hadn't given up a hit. That was the good news for the young pitcher. The bad news was that the game was still scoreless.

As we approached the ninth inning and Alvarez still had his no hitter intact, I began to realize I had never been in this position before. We could have a pitcher throw nine no-hit innings, but his team had not scored. So the possibility existed that this game could go to extra innings.

During the commercial break after the eighth inning, I said to our producer, Mark Iacofano, "This is bizarre, but it's not officially a no-hitter unless Alvarez finishes the game."

In order for that to happen, his team would need to score a run in the bottom of the ninth. But first he needed to set down the Tigers in the top of the inning. The good news for him is that Detroit didn't put up much of a fight.

Alex Avila swung at the second pitch of the inning and hit a grounder back to the mound. Don Kelly swung at the first pitch he saw and did the same. With two outs, Andy Dirks worked a walk, but Matt Tuiasosopo flailed weakly at a 3–2 pitch. Alvarez had retired 27 batters without allowing a hit.

The crowd cheered wildly, and Alvarez raised his hands in triumph. It seemed as if he actually thought Miami was winning, and he had the no-hitter. Yes, he had nine no-hit innings, but there was nothing to really celebrate yet.

Luke Putkonen relieved Porcello in the bottom of the ninth, and after retiring the first batter, Putkonen gave up singles to Giancarlo Stanton and Logan Morrison. Putkonen got the next batter, then a wild pitch and a walk loaded the bases. This was where a weird story got even weirder.

Pinch hitter Greg Dobbs stepped to the plate. And the on-deck batter was none other than the guy throwing the no-hitter—Alvarez! Putkonen uncorked his second wild pitch of the inning, Stanton scored, and the celebration began. Alvarez had his no-hitter, the Marlins got the win, and nobody got the game-winning RBI.

There have been more exciting no-hitters, and there have been more dominant ones. But I'm pretty sure that I'll never see a stranger no-hitter in my broadcasting career.

CHAPTER 8
MANAGERS

The Skippers

Over 25-plus years of broadcasting baseball, I've had the privilege to work with a long list of the game's most interesting and talented managers. The interaction has been fascinating, and I've learned a great deal from each man. Here's a list of some of my most memorable managers.

Jim Tracy: One of my earliest minor league jobs was broadcasting for the Cubs Class A affiliate in Peoria, Illinois, in 1987. The manager that year was former Chicago Cub Jim Tracy, who would go on to manage the Dodgers, Pirates, and Rockies in the major leagues.

Tracy played briefly in the big leagues for the Cubs in 1980 and 1981, and he actually had his number retired in Wrigley. That's right, No. 23 will hang forever in Chicago. Of course, it's actually because the guy who inherited the number was Ryne Sandberg, the best second baseman of his era and a member of baseball's Hall of Fame.

Tracy may not have been a great player, but he was a riot to work with. I've yet to come across anyone in the game who can tell a story like Trace. One "Trac-ism" that comes to mind was what he would often say about the National Anthem: "Every time I heard that song, I had a bad game."

We had such a good relationship that I could say anything to him and not offend him. In 1988, the Peoria club got off to a horrible start. After a particularly tough loss, Tracy said, "Don't worry. I saw some good things tonight. We're about to bust out of it."

"Don't count on it," I said.

To which Tracy replied, "Mario, I hope all of your kids grow up to have the same nose you've got."

Touché.

Marcel Lachemann: Lach was the manager of the California Angels when I first got to the big leagues as a broadcaster in 1995. A quiet, stoic presence, Marcel was easy to work with.

As a longtime coach, nothing seemed to bother him. He had seen and experienced it all. This tranquility came in handy when his 1995 Angels collapsed, blowing an 11-game lead in August to miss the playoffs.

As the world was caving in on the Angels, Lachemann took all of the criticism and heat with class. The following season he stepped down, admitting he could no longer motivate his team.

The thing I remember most about this longtime baseball man is that he treated me like a veteran broadcaster and not as a young kid trying to find his way as a big-league broadcaster. Win or lose, Lach was always the same, and it's something I have always appreciated.

Terry Collins: With the Angels, Collins' press conferences were often entertaining. The manager didn't have time for "dumb" questions, and he would let reporters know it. You definitely had to be on your toes during those sessions.

Edgy is best way I can describe Collins. A native Michigander, Collins is from Midland and starred collegiately at Eastern Michigan. Collins has a reputation around the game as an intense competitor, one who sometimes couldn't turn off his emotions. There certainly is that side of him, but he's also an ultra-intelligent baseball mind who has mellowed over the years.

But the other side is the loyalty he shows his friends. Collins had a place in Tampa, and each season he would us invite to a dinner party when the Angels played the Rays. Collins had a relationship with the great Sandy Koufax from his days working in the Dodgers' farm system.

At dinner I was walking around, chatting with the guests, when I noticed a familiar-looking man and decided to introduce myself. I couldn't place him, so I decided to try to find out who he was. As I introduced myself, he stuck his hand out and said, "Hi, I'm Sandy Koufax. Pleasure to meet you."

Umm, I'm an idiot. I was literally speechless. It was awkward from that point forward as I struggled not to make a boob of myself.

The next day I stopped into Terry's office at the ballpark to thank him for inviting me to the dinner and to tell him I met Koufax and how star-struck I was.

Terry deadpanned, "Yeah, it looked like you crapped your pants."

Before he took over as the manager of the Mets, Terry would always tune in to Tigers games when he visited his home in Midland during the summer.

Joe Maddon: Baseball fans know Maddon as one of the best managers in the game, the man who turned Tampa from a laughingstock into a perennial playoff contender.

I got to know Joe early in my career. Back in the late 1980s, I interacted with Joe when he was a roving instructor and I was broadcasting in the minors with the Quad City Angels. He's one of the most personable guys around. He's also very intelligent and the ultimate outside-the-box thinker.

Maddon has always been different from any other manager. As a bench coach with the Angels, he would post the lineup card every day with a motivational saying attached. Some players would scoff and laugh, but the messages did make you think.

Joe was one of those guys you just knew would someday be a big-league manager. The thing that I most admire about him is that he's his own man. When he took over the Angels in mid-1999, the one thing I noticed is that his personality never changed. The pressures increased, but his personality never wavered.

One incident that taught me how much confidence Maddon had in himself was in September of that year. The Angels had a day game in Minnesota, and a University of Minnesota Golden Gophers football game was scheduled later in the day at the Metrodome,

To give his team a bit of a breather, Maddon ran out a lineup of B-teamers for the 11:00 AM start against the Twins' Eric Milton. Gone from the lineup that day were names like Jim Edmonds, Mo Vaughn, Tim Salmon, Darin Erstad, and Garret Anderson. The veterans were getting the day off because of the morning start.

As Eric Milton took a no-hitter late in the game, Maddon stuck to his guns and kept his veterans on the bench. He had promised them the day off. Now keep in mind, this was a guy who was auditioning for a major league job. This might have been his only shot.

Maddon believed so fiercely in what he was doing that the veteran players all watched as Milton fired a no-hitter. The easy choice for Joe would have been to send out his big bats as pinch hitters, but a man's word is his word and Maddon never wavered, despite knowing the fallout would be sizable if his team failed to get a hit with his starters on the bench.

The Man Behind the Growl

Jim Leyland is the epitome of the old-school baseball managers. He is gruffness personified. He's old fashioned, he smokes, and he tells it like it is. Jim Leyland also might be the most misunderstood manager in recent memory.

Unlike Joe Torre, Jim wasn't a great player. Unlike Bobby Valentine, he was never a hot-shot prospect. Jim Leyland spent seven seasons playing in the minor leagues, never rising above AA. Then he spent 10 more years managing in the minors. This is a guy who paid his dues.

There's no question that "Skip" has his own way of dealing with things. When the team struggles, he accepts full responsibility. When the team wins, Jim is the guy who is always making sure to mention all 25 players—and everyone else in the organization. Love him or hate him, nobody will ever say Jim is a phony.

Jim had a hugely successful run in Pittsburgh, then he won a World Series with the Marlins (and general manager Dave Dombrowski). Jim stuck through one year of a fire sale there, then he left for greener pastures in Colorado.

While managing a bad Rockies team, Jim realized something. He was no longer "all-in." Yes, he did the best he could, but the fire was gone. Playing in the thin air of Colorado, it was like managing what amounted to arena baseball. Leyland resigned, walking away from two more years on his contract and $4 million.

What people don't see beyond the gruff exterior is the caring family guy who values relationships. There have been several times when I've shown up at the park and Jim would rather talk about my family than last night's game. It sounds simple, but Jim realizes what's important. Yes, there have been a few expletive-laced tirades in his office, but there have also been moments where he's advised me about my son's baseball experiences.

The way he values relationships is obvious in his managerial style. While losses tear him up inside, he'll do his best to keep his players loose. National baseball analyst Tim Kurkjian said recently that he's never seen a team carry out its manager's message more than the Tigers.

And he has a bit of a theatrical side, as well. There are several stories about Jim breaking into song at a party. As rough as his voice is when he's mad, it's surprisingly not too bad when he croons one of his favorites. But there is one visual I'll never forget.

A couple years ago, the Tigers were dragging on the day after a night game in Toronto. Away from the cameras, Jim is liable to say or do just about anything. When he's sitting on his couch, he may be wearing a T-shirt or nothing but his baseball pants. On this day, Jim decided to channel his inner Michael Jackson. Seeing the skipper moonwalking in his underwear brought instant life to the clubhouse.

Of course, the moment everybody in Detroit still talks about happened in September 2011. The Tigers were comfortably ahead in the AL Central Division, so it was not a question of if they would clinch their first division title since 1987…it was a question of when.

The Tigers were in Oakland for a four-game series. After losing Thursday night, Doug Fister (one of the finest mid-season acquisition in the last 20 years) threw eight innings, allowing only three hits. Jose Valverde continued his perfect season, and the Tigers were division champions.

The locker room celebration was crazy but under control. FS Detroit carried the whole thing live, and it was great television. After getting drenched with champagne, I made my way to the manager's office. It might have been Jim's finest moment.

When I found him, he was choked up—not just about the division title but about what it meant to the city of Detroit. He talked about how important this was for the fans, the people who have gone through rough times. Lots of coaches and/or managers talk that way, but few really mean it like Jim did. Jim displayed a lot of raw emotion that night.

The next season, the Tigers would clinch their second consecutive Central Division crown, this time in Kansas City. Again, my job was to interview the skipper. It was almost a carbon copy of the previous season. Once again Leyland teared up, reflecting on his team's accomplishments and the joy it would bring to the city.

I quickly became known as the only guy who could make Jim Leyland cry.

———

Manager Jim Leyland hits grounders to infielders during a baseball workout at Fenway Park in Boston on Friday, October 11, 2013. The Tigers faced the Boston Red Sox in Game 1 of the American League Championship Series the next day. *(AP Photo/ Charlie Riedel)*

The celebration in 2011 was certainly special, and the celebration in 2012 was great, too. By the time the team clinched their third straight division title, you had to figure it would be old hat.

After being swept in the previous year's World Series, 2013 was a year with huge expectations. It was world championship or bust. The division-clinching celebration came a few days later than normal. Despite winning two of three against Chicago, the Tigers couldn't put away the stubborn Cleveland Indians. So they traveled to Minnesota and promptly fell to the Twins in the series opener before winning the second game. It was still a matter of when they would clinch, not if, but the season-ending trip to Miami would be much sweeter with the division wrapped up.

Max Scherzer picked up his 21st win, and the Tigers were Central Division champions for a third straight season thanks to a 1–0 shutout. Now it was time to party. The celebration was respectful but still emotional. This team has its eyes on a bigger prize, but this was worth some (non-alcoholic) bubbly, to be sure.

As has become a nice tradition, I had the chance to interview Leyland in the relative quiet of his office. If there was any doubt about the emotional toll of the season, it quickly disappeared.

"We talked in spring training [that] this was a tough year for the guys because the expectations were so high, it's almost like we were set up to fail," Leyland said, tears running down his face. "From day one of spring training, I told them.... I told them don't get caught up in the expectations—get caught up in how we're going to live up to those expectations, and I think that's what they've done."

Now the skipper was having trouble finishing his sentences. "And I want to say thank you to the fans. I'm so proud of what you've done for our ball club, and what you've done for me since I've been here...and I just hope that you feel like you're getting your money's worth because we try to entertain you, and you keep coming out. I can't tell you what that means to us. It's like a sixth man."

In the middle of this deeply emotional moment, we were interrupted. Torii Hunter gave his manager a hug and carried him back into the main clubhouse. There Jim was doused with champagne. Then the fans got a brief glimpse of Jim Leyland, unfiltered, as the manager moonwalked off stage right and back into his office.

Once he dried himself off, Jim slid back behind the microphone and finished his thoughts.

"Your front office, they never get any credit. Behind the scenes, they do a lot of preparation to make the operation work, and I'd like to thank them, all of our scouts, our minor league people.... It's a nice marriage, it really is, but most of all those fans.... It's been unbelievable."

Another September, another emotional Leyland interview. It's become a nice tradition.

My Lineup Is My Lineup

You've heard the cliché over and over: "The season is a marathon, not a sprint." This is true in all team sports, but none more so than baseball. Nearly two months and 30-plus games of spring training, 162 regular season games over six months, and if the team is lucky, a few weeks of playoffs. And consider that we're talking about nine innings every day, at least 2½ hours a pop. That's a lot of baseball.

Players talk about the dog days of August, but these guys get tired more than us fans ever know. It's not like a five-day, 40-hour work week for them. So it makes sense that guys need the occasional day off, whether it's for physical or mental reasons. At least it should make sense.

Yet as much as you try to explain the difficulties of navigating through a season, fans don't want to hear it when it comes to resting players. Part of it makes sense. If a family comes to a game, they expect to see Miguel Cabrera and Austin Jackson. (Fortunately, these are players who play nearly every game.)

If you want to tick off Jim Leyland, try walking into his office on a hot summer day in the middle of a pennant race and ask him why he is resting one of his regulars. The skipper has been prickly over the years when fans and media have questioned his lineup, and I don't blame him.

The battle occurs every season. The Tigers are facing a must-win, and everyone goes crazy when the skipper sits one of his guys. If he's said it once, he's said it a million times: "My lineup is my lineup—end of story."

That's code for, "How many times do I have to tell you people that all players need rest from time to time?"

As well-informed as fans and media are these days, we are not managers. Leyland is privy to inside information on the mental and physical health of his players. He knows about every sore hamstring, every crispy back, and every tired arm. That's why he meets with his staff (and usually the players) every day. Information is power.

In 2009, Leyland rested second baseman Placido Polanco in the heat of a pennant race against the Minnesota Twins. When the Tigers lost a key game down the stretch, it was open season on the skipper.

What everyone didn't know at the time was that Polly was running on fumes, nursing a myriad of nagging injuries. Putting a fresh Ramon Santiago out there instead of an exhausted Polanco was clearly the smart move, no matter what the results. But without that information, it looked like a roll of the dice.

Sometimes fans don't want to hear it. They always make the salary argument. "These guys are making millions of dollars, so they should play every day." But what nobody ever says is this—making more money doesn't make you a better player, and the checkbook doesn't give you the superpower to heal your body.

It's ironic and convenient that nobody mentions that one of the big reasons the Tigers pulled away late in 2011 and 2012 was because they were rested. Both years resulted in division championships.

The benefits to Leyland's approach is twofold. First, players are more honest with the training and coaching staff about when they need a day off rather than pushing through it when they really shouldn't. Second, the players know the skipper has their back. He's not going to second-guess them or hang them out to dry. Leyland has always been known as a players' manager, and that's part of the reason he's going to the Hall of Fame.

Just to give you some perspective, in 2012, only one Tigers player played in all 162 games, and that was Prince Fielder, making him one of only four players to appear in every game: Fielder, Starlin Castro, Adam Jones, and Ichiro Suzuki. In addition, Miguel Cabrera has only played in less than 160 games once in his Tigers career—when the team shut him down in 2010 with a sore ankle and the team wasn't heading anywhere.

There are few true workhorses that can literally play every day and produce results at the same time.

Leyland has always been known as a players' manager. His guys will run through a wall for him—and that's part of the reason he's going to the Hall of Fame.

CHAPTER 9

LIFE IN THE BOOTH

On the Road Again

When you travel around the major leagues for nearly 20 seasons, you can't help but notice some of the intricacies of each ballpark. Yes, each stadium has its nooks and crannies in the field of play, but I'm talking about the important details. Who has the best media dinner spreads? Which stadiums have a bathroom close to the booth? Which locker rooms have all the bells and whistles?

And then, yes, there are factors that actually come into play on the field. In the mid-1980s, for example, the Kansas City Royals and St. Louis Cardinals stressed speed, and their parks fit their style of play (and vice-versa), with fast artificial surfaces that allowed them to play "small ball." The Red Sox have always been a team full of sluggers, which fits the cozy dimensions of Fenway Park.

Which parks are the toughest on the visiting team?

Here are my top five toughest places to visit, both as a broadcaster and for the Tigers.

5. Oakland Coliseum. First, you've got that cold, damp night air, which makes you feel like you're in a fog. It's hard to believe that this is an organization that won three consecutive World Series titles in the 1970s, three straight American League pennants in the 1980s and 1990s, and had one of the best records in the game during the early 2000s. Hollywood even based a movie (2011's *Moneyball*, starring Brad Pitt) on their general manager.

That's why it's sad that the Coliseum is such a lonely place during home games. Oakland has always been known for the crazy Raiders fans—and believe me, I'm glad not to be broadcasting from the "black hole." But right now, for baseball, the Coliseum has little energy except for the booming PA system and the blasting music between innings. It's no wonder the team is hoping to move to San Jose. Because of the lack of fans, the sound system feels even louder than it should. We wear headsets designed to block out noise, but they don't work in Oakland.

Batters hate hitting here because there are approximately 10 miles of foul territory, so low-scoring games are pretty common. And because the Raiders are co-inhabitants, the field looks like a sand lot by September.

4. Coors Field (Denver). When the Rockies began play in 1993, their home games were like arena baseball. The thin air bolstered the careers of guys like Larry Walker, Vinny Castilla, and Dante Bichette. It also scared the living daylights out of any decent pitcher.

In 2002, the Rox decided that enough was enough, and they began storing their baseballs in a humidor before the game. This did help, but no lead is ever safe at Coors. Some managers get psyched out by the conditions and can't handle their staffs.

3. Fenway Park (Boston). When you come to Fenway, either as an announcer or as a player, you'd better pack a lunch—and maybe dinner— because this ain't going to be a quick one.

The Red Sox and Yankees are known for taking pitches to wear down the other team's starters. You can't argue with the results because they have been two of the winningest teams in baseball. But it sure makes for a long day at the office.

On the field, visitors need a GPS to navigate the quirky cutouts and corners. Of course, there's the Green Monster (pronounced "Monstah" if you're from New England), which is 37'2" of uniqueness. If a player hits a shot to left, he'd better keep running because there's a good chance it's going to bounce off the Monster. You really have to poke one to clear the wall. In 2003, the Sox added "Monster seats" so fans can sit right on top of the wall, yelling down at the visitors.

On both the left- and right-field lines, the seats jet out, creating an asymmetrical stadium. Even the most experienced fielders can get twisted and turned around. Just ask former Indian Kenny Lofton, whose misplay helped the Red Sox win Game 7 of the 2007 American League Championship Series.

Leading or trailing, opposing players dread the seventh-inning stretch. That's when "it" comes, no matter what. Neil Diamond's "Sweet Caroline" gets the fans involved, and it can be the most annoying song in the history of recorded music, especially if your team is losing.

2. The Metrodome (Minneapolis). Fake turf, a dome, and garbage bags in the outfield. Those are what come to mind when thinking about the former home of the Minnesota Twins. Again, this stadium was built for the

Twins—they've always been fast, and great on defense, but this dome of doom really looked more like a practice facility.

Visiting outfielders always had trouble, losing balls in the opaque roof, and once a ball hit the turf, it was off to the races.

Some of the strangest things would happen in that place. Late leads almost always seemed to disappear. A misplayed ball always started a winning rally. These days it is a much more pleasant visit to Minneapolis thanks to Target Field, which is the new home of the Twins.

1. Old Yankee Stadium (New York). Let me start by saying that the new Yankee Stadium is beautiful. It is shiny, comfortable, and majestic in a manner befitting the sport's trademark team. The simple fact is, however, that everything the new stadium is, the old stadium was not.

For a team that has won 27 championships, you would think their home would be a cathedral. And yes, the monuments in centerfield were awesome, and the upper deck was magical. But that's where it ended.

The fans are the most knowledgeable in baseball (just ask them), but they are some of the most gruff people I've ever encountered.

One time after a Yankees loss, I saw former Yankees reliever Jeff Nelson leaving the stadium with his wife and young child. That didn't stop the fans from cursing him on the way out—and he played for the home team!

The new stadium is sparkling clean, really immaculate. It has great sightlines, and it's a terrific place to watch the game. The old stadium, though, was intimidating. You felt the history of the organization the minute you walked into the ballpark. From the monuments to the overhang, which seemed to hover over the entire field, the old Yankee Stadium had a feeling all its own.

Listen and Learn

Smart young players learn from the older guys. Every team has guys who love to just sit around and talk about baseball. Whether it's an all-time great like Al Kaline or a guy who's seen it all like Torii Hunter, there's nothing better than baseball talk. The smart youngsters get it. Curtis Granderson did that during his time with the Tigers, and I'm sure he soaked in knowledge from the likes of Derek Jeter and Mariano Rivera during his time with the Yankees.

It's the same for announcers. No matter how long you've been in the business, you never know it all. One of the best listeners I've ever encountered was Ernie Harwell. Enough said.

I find it fascinating to listen to other announcers around the game. It gives me a better picture of where I stand and what I need to improve on. One thing about broadcasting is that it's totally subjective. Two people can broadcast the same game but be received very differently. Plus, there's an old adage that there's no such thing as an original idea—they're all stolen. So where better to mine for ideas than by listening to other people doing the same thing?

All announcers have their favorite idols from the past. For me, it was Ernie, Paul Carey, and George Kell. There's no question that listening to them for so many years helped shape me into the announcer I am today. But I also think it's important to listen to your contemporaries. What have they found success with? What are some of their struggles?

I have made many great friends in the business over the years, and leaning on them has helped me tremendously. You truly can learn something from everyone in the business. When I was in the minor leagues, current A's announcer Vince Cotroneo had just gotten his first big-league job with the Astros. I was fortunate enough to take over for Vince in Triple A Tucson. We instantly became friends. Vince was always a guy I looked up to because he took the time to help me by answering my endless questions and welcoming me to the big-league scene when I got my first major league job with the Angels. I learned what it was like to be a pro from Vince and how to carry myself at this level.

His current partner in Oakland is Ken Korach. The voice of the A's and I go back to our days together in the Pacific Coast league. I have always had a tremendous amount of respect for Ken's skill. He has a great voice and a strong ability to master the pace of the game, which are things I admire. There are certain times when you want to get excited, and other times when you need to slow down. He has mastered both. Throw in the fact that he is a quality person, and I'm proud to be his friend. He is someone all young announcers should learn from.

Cleveland's Tom Hamilton is one of a kind. Eventually, he will be in the Hall of Fame. Tom has been a great mentor to me and Tigers radio voice Dan Dickerson. Dan and I always talk about how Tom is willing to share information to make us better announcers and more informed about the business. Tom is also always willing to help the young guys. You can ask him anything, even bounce ideas off of him, and Tom is always there for you.

As far as his performance, his ability to capture the exciting moments in the game is second to none. Walk-off home run? Nobody calls it better than Tom. Yes, the Indians have had some great teams, but they've also had quite a few losing ones. Through wins or losses, Tom has an innate ability to make the drama come alive.

Everyone has that one friend in the business who is always a phone call away, a true confidant. For me, it's former Angels, Brewers, and Diamondbacks announcer Daron Sutton. Daron is only the second most famous member of his family since his father, Don, won 324 games during a Hall of Fame career. Daron spent one season playing in the minors before deciding to make his name in broadcasting.

"Sutt" and I became partners on Angels radio in 2000, and we have been close friends ever since. It is invaluable to have that one guy you can call for advice to get you through the tough times in the business. And I always try to be there when he calls me. Daron is the hardest worker I have met, but he also taught me a valuable lesson in the booth. It's just baseball, so it's okay to have some fun.

Jinxes and Curses

Baseball fans come in all shapes and sizes. Men, women, different races, religions—we all love the game. Most of these fans are pretty logical. I mean, when the manager brings in his lefty reliever to face a left-handed slugger, it's "by the book." The game even has unwritten rules.

Except when it comes to announcers, that is.

When the Tigers play the Yankees in the playoffs, it doesn't matter who calls the game—New York fans think the announcers are pro-Tigers, and Detroit fans say they're pro-Yankees. That's just a fact.

The good news is that most fans realize that there is no jinx. Whatever is going to happen happens, regardless of what we say. But it still makes for some interesting coincidences.

Like in 2012, when Max Scherzer was dominating the Twins. It wasn't more than a few seconds after I said, "Max Scherzer is cruising. He's retired 13 straight…", when, of course, Denard Span hits his first home run of the year.

"Thanks, Mario," the Twitter world responded.

Or in Oakland, when Josh Reddick came to the plate against Rick Porcello. "Here's Reddick," I started. "He has good power, but Rick should be able to use his sinker to get a ground ball." Next pitch—bang! Home run. Yup, it's all my fault.

I don't believe in a jinx, and I never will. Yet you can't convince some fans that it just isn't logical.

Now when you're talking about a no-hitter, that's a bit different. I've been fortunate enough to be at the mic for both of Justin Verlander's masterpieces. Several fans have asked me the question, "If you don't believe in jinxes, why didn't you actually say 'no-hitter' when you were broadcasting them?"

That's a very legitimate question. I believe that it is more about baseball etiquette than a jinx.

All sports have weird, sometimes crazy, superstitions. Some players never step on the foul line when taking or leaving the field. Hall of Famer Wade Boggs would run at 7:17 every game night, and he'd always eat chicken for dinner.

One of baseball's most famous superstitions is that when a guy is throwing a no-hitter, usually by about the fifth inning, his teammates won't sit next to him on the bench or talk to him. If you're broadcasting a game, or just being a fan at a no-no, you aren't supposed to mention the no-hitter.

I might say something like, "Justin is really dealing, and the Blue Jays can't touch him." Or I could ask for a shot of the scoreboard showing no hits, but that's it. Of course, I can't make Justin give up a hit, but it's better to be safe than sorry, right?

I always find it amusing how some fans harp on the jinxes, but when I say, "Miguel Cabrera has owned pitcher (fill in the blank)", and then he hits a home run, nobody mentions it. Funny how that works.

Baseball is certainly a game of jinxes and curses. From the Babe Ruth haunting the Red Sox to a billy goat causing the Cubs more than 100 years of futility, there's always something. The Angels had bad luck in the 1980s because Angel Stadium was built on an ancient Indian burial ground.

Or so they say.

And the Indians finished last in the late 1980s because *Sports Illustrated* said they were the best team in baseball.

Accuse me of jinxing a player all you want—I'll never believe it.

The Grind

One term used in baseball more than any other sport is "the Grind." Every season as summer kicks in and the temperatures rise, you'll hear players and managers always talk about the Grind. When you play 162 games in a span of approximately 180 days, it really is a grind.

My one wish for all baseball fans would be to let them travel with a major league team for a full season to get an appreciation of how difficult it can be to mentally and physically survive the marathon that is a major league season.

Many people say, "Yeah, well, they get paid millions of dollars. They shouldn't have any worries. I'd sign up for that right now!"

Well, it is true that players earn more in one or two years than most people make in an entire lifetime. And "earn" is the operative word.

There's no question that players live a life of privilege. They cash a huge paycheck, they travel first class, stay in the best hotels, and eat at the best restaurants. They also have folks like clubhouse attendants to take care of some of their errands.

But think about a guy like Tigers utilityman Don Kelly. Out of a 4½-month season, Don is away from his two small children for weeks at a time. It's hard to put a price tag on something like that.

From mid-February to October. the dedication it takes to be a major league player is incredible. Sure, they get to sleep late, but then they go to work, sometimes in 95-degree temperatures and sometimes for 20 days in a row. These guys travel in different time zones. There have been times when guys wake up in the morning and don't realize where they are.

Ivan Rodriguez smiles during a break in the action of a game against the Seattle Mariners on Friday, July 7, 2006, at Safeco Field in Seattle. Even All-Star catchers deal with a lot of physical ailments during the grind of a full season. *(AP Photo/Ted S. Warren)*

Oh, and don't forget spring training. Yes, a trip to Florida or Arizona sounds like fun, and there is less stress for those six weeks, but it is still work.

Don't get me wrong—these guys have a great life. It certainly does not compare to a construction worker who puts in long hot hours during the summer. Nor does the stress compare to a family struggling financially to pay the bills and meet the mortgage.

But with all of these conditions come constant job reviews from fans, announcers, coaches, managers, and team executives. It's clear this is a high-pressure but high-reward tightrope.

For most players it is a constant battle to prove yourself every single day. When you do get a day off, many times it is spent on a plane, traveling to the next city. There are no Fourth of July picnics with the family. There is always a game. No sleeping in on Sundays. There's always a game. No weekend getaways up north. There's always a game. Families are separated, and kids usually only see Dad on television. First day of school? Sorry, Dad is in Seattle.

I'm not sure what is more taxing—the physical part of the game or the mental part.

Take catchers, for instance. Imagine spending day after day, squatting with all of that gear. It's incredible to think that Ivan "Pudge" Rodriguez caught more than 20,000 innings during his soon-to-be Hall of Fame career. It was 18,000 innings for Carlton Fisk. In addition to the squatting, there are foul tips off various body parts and massive collisions at the plate. And that doesn't even take into account what catchers deal with when they're at bat.

There were many times I'd see Pudge in the clubhouse, all black and blue from the night before, only to strap everything back on and go out there for another day at the office.

I've never seen a catcher take more of a beating than Alex Avila did in 2011. This guy was a walking bruise from head to toe, not to mention his battered knees. Alex played every game, never asking for a night off. Even as his production at the plate suffered, he literally took one for the team, and his teammates noticed.

When you look at Prince Fielder, you may not think of an athlete, but this guy plays every day. He's never missed more than five games in a season. Ichiro Suzuki came to America at the age of 27. For the next 11 seasons, the

5'11", 170-lb. batting machine missed an average of three games a season. I guess they come in all sizes.

Life isn't quite as hard on us announcers. After all, it's not like we're playing the game. Our main challenge is mental. Sure, it's easy to get up for the big games when there's maybe a battle for first place or someone going for their 20th win. But it's the mid-August games in Kansas City that can wear you down. On nights like that, you know it's going to be a long night as soon as you speak your first words on the air.

Just like players, we can't possibly bring our "A" game every night. That doesn't mean we don't try, but it's just not doable. You just try to be as consistent as you can.

My bosses at FOX have asked me from time to time if I want to take a meaningless series off, but I always refuse. I appreciate their asking, I really do, but I've waited all my life for this job. Being the voice of the Tigers is a responsibility I take very seriously. I've made a deal with the fans—if they watch (or even if they don't), I'll be there.

Nervous Energy

If you ask most ballplayers about their first game, they'll be able to tell you everything about it, such as the opponent, the situation when they came up to bat, or the moment they took the mound for the first time. Most players remember it like it was yesterday.

For broadcasters, everyone remembers his first game. My first big-league broadcast was on April 26, 1995. Remember, the 1995 season was shortened as the end result of the 1994 strike, which canceled the World Series for the first time. The players were pumped up, and so was I.

The team that hired me, the (then) Anaheim Angels, was taking on the team I've rooted for my entire life, the Detroit Tigers. Chuck Finley started against Mike Moore. The Tigers led 3–2 in the eighth when Cecil Fielder clobbered a two-run homer for a three-run lead. The bullpen held off an Angels rally and won 5–4. One of my coolest memories that day was getting to interview Sparky Anderson for our pregame show.

Of course, there is one other thing I remember about that game. I was probably the most nervous I have ever been.

It wasn't like I hadn't paid my dues. I spent eight seasons in the minor leagues and had more than 1,000 games under my belt. I kept telling myself that baseball is baseball, the game is the same, and I was ready. But there's no question about it—this was not just another game.

Just like a rookie player, I had finally made the show. No more long bus rides to Peoria, Illinois, or Davenport, Iowa. No more pulling the tarp when it rained and selling advertising packages to clients. This was the big leagues.

As much as I told myself I was ready, there was definitely a little part of me that wondered if that was true. Now, instead of a few hundred listeners, there would be thousands. That's a lot more ears tuned in and a lot more pressure.

Thankfully, my big-league debut went smoothly, but as I've learned, those nerves never completely go away. Every year, the first telecast, even in spring training, is a challenge. I always do my research, but did I do enough? Am I up to speed on all of the new players, the new storylines?

It's almost like I have to prove to myself that I can still do this every spring. My guess is that when I stop getting excited about it, that's when it's time to walk away.

———

Nervous energy is one thing, but occasionally during my career I've been susceptible to panic attacks. It's not something I've talked about to many people—just a select few fellow announcers. Thankfully, I've learned that I'm definitely not the only broadcaster that this has happened to.

One moment that sticks out for me happened in New York in August 2007. The Tigers had just finished a series in Cleveland and were headed to the Big Apple to face the Yankees while tied for first in the AL Central.

Going to New York, especially at the old Yankee Stadium, was a big deal. With a first-place ball club, everything was magnified.

Justin Verlander was on the mound for the Tigers, and the pennant race was in full swing. I was just doing my normal preparation, going through a routine I'd done thousands of times. I finished my pregame dinner and headed to the booth to finish filling out my scorecard and rehearse the opening to our telecast. Yes, this was a huge game, but I was excited, not nervous.

Rod and I were ready, so our producer began to run though our rehearsal. We looked over the video elements that we would discuss to set up the game. Then it happened. About two minutes before going on the air—going live— my mind went completely blank. I couldn't remember any elements of our open. My heart began to race, and I began to panic. Airtime was less than 120 seconds away, and I was about to make a complete fool of myself.

As we get closer to the show, our producer will always count us down— one minute to air, 30 seconds, etc. While this was happening, I desperately asked him to recap the elements. Here we are, with 30 seconds to air, and our producer is quickly recapping the open.

"We're talking about Verlander and how he has gotten stronger as the season has progressed—20 seconds. The Tigers are tied with Cleveland for first place. And we're on in 10, 9, 8…"

We were going on the air in seconds, and my mind was still totally blank. It was the most panicked I had ever been in my career. Verlander, the Yankees, Yankee Stadium, a pennant race—it all raced through my mind, not to mention the number of viewers we would have for a marquee game.

As we opened the broadcast, I was somehow able to remember that Verlander would be the first element of our open. My heart was beating so fast that I was almost out of breath. I really didn't know if I would make it through the entire open.

This felt like it was my first broadcast. I was overwhelmed by the pressure. I really wanted to call for a commercial break, but that was not an option. Somehow I stumbled through the rest of the open in one piece, and then it was over. I wondered what had just happened and if it made any sense at all.

From that point forward I have made it a point to make sure all of my producers walk me through the elements just before airtime. Most nights it's overkill and I don't need it. You just never know when you might.

In more than 25 years on the air, I've had maybe three panic attacks like this. Why they happen is a mystery. I think it's mostly the mental fatigue of doing as many games as we do. Fortunately, I've survived each time, and now I know how to deal with them. But that doesn't make them any less confusing.

The Corner

When is newer not better?

We all like new stuff, whether it's the new iPhone or the latest in HD TV. But there are times when the classics are still appreciated.

One of the big trends in baseball is the building of new stadiums. In the last few years, there have been new parks built for the Twins, the Mets, and even the Yankees. The House that Ruth Built is no more; it has been replaced by the new Yankee Stadium. Sure, the new parks have all the amenities, and they look really cool on TV. But to me, they have nothing on classics like Fenway Park and Wrigley Field.

There aren't too many old-school parks left in the game. For a kid growing up in Detroit, the ultimate old-school park was Tiger Stadium. It really was a cathedral in the game.

For almost 90 years, baseball was played at the corner of Michigan and Trumbull. Tiger Stadium opened in back in 1912, and by the time the Tigers left for Comerica Park in 2000, they had left behind decades of some of the greatest memories in baseball history.

You look at the rubble now, and it's hard to believe the memories that were born there, including Babe Ruth's 700th home run in 1934, Lou Gehrig's 2,130[th] straight and last big-league game, and Denny McLain's 30th win in 1968. I'll never forget a young rookie with long curly hair named Mark Fidrych who captured the heart of a nation when he knocked off the mighty Yankees on national television in 1976. And how many times have we seen the video of Sparky Anderson telling Kirk Gibson, "He don't want to pitch to you," then Gibby crushing the home run off Rich "Goose" Gossage to wrap up the 1984 World Series.

Growing up in Detroit, I spent many summer nights as a fan in the seats at the grand old park, imagining that someday I could play for the Tigers. That never happened, but in 1995 I got my first chance to live another dream, and that was to call a game from Tiger Stadium. I was broadcasting for the Angels, and our first trip to Detroit was on July 13. The Angels would win 8–5 with three runs in the tenth, but to me, the game really didn't matter. I remember more about the sights and sounds of the park and how it compared to my memories as a kid.

You know how when you visit the school you attended as a kid how small everything looks? That's what it was like for me. The clubhouses were tiny! How could 25 fully grown men fit in there? It was the same thing with the dugouts. I remember watching guys pacing, spitting, cheering on their teammates, but now…well, I don't know how anyone could move. Still, to think that I was in the same place that some of the all-time greats dressed and sat— that was unforgettable.

The view from the radio booth was the best in the game. We were so close to the action that you could actually hear the catcher talk to the batter or umpire. The center-field wall was 440' from home plate, and it seemed like a mile and a half from our view in the booth.

Over the years, broadcasters learned the tricks of the trade at Tiger Stadium. Ernie Harwell used to work with a screen in front of the booth because foul balls would scream into the booth otherwise. In what you would call the home-field advantage, the visiting booth had no protection, and all it took was one foul ball flying by your ear to put you on the defensive.

I walked into Sparky Anderson's office for his pregame meeting with the press thinking, *Wow, I had no idea how small his office was.* Sparky sat at his desk, answering questions through the smoke of his pipe, kind of like I'd imagine a grandfather sitting at his chair reading *The Night Before Christmas.*

I was also amazed at how friendly everyone was. It was a real sense of community. I remember longtime Tigers radio engineer Howard Stitzel bringing donuts into the booth to make the visiting broadcast crew feel welcome.

Yes, it's part of growing up; everything seems smaller. As cavernous as Tiger Stadium seemed to me as a child, it was so much smaller as a broadcaster. It was less intimidating, but the experience was far more rewarding. Calling a game at Tigers Stadium was like dream.

It was the same park where as a kid I would sit in the right-field overhang seats so I could yell at Dwight Evans, Dave Winfield, or any other right fielder who came to visit.

"Hey, Evans! You suck!' I would yell.

I'll bet he never heard that one before.

I remember the footage of last game at Tiger Stadium like it was yesterday.

Ernie Harwell put it best:

> Ladies and gentlemen, less than six months ago, we began a warm season of farewells, and with each passing day we came a little bit closer to this historic occasion. The Lions, Joe Louis, and Nelson Mandela. Six-thousand eight-hundred and seventy-three regular-season games, 35 postseason contests, and a trio of spectacular All-Star Games, Tiger Stadium has been home to this great game of baseball. But more than anything, it has been a cherished home to our memories. Will you remember that last base hit? The last out? How about that last pitch? Or maybe it's the first time as a child when you saw that green, green grass that will forever be etched into your mind and soul. Tonight, we say good-bye. But we will not forget. Open your eyes, look around, and take a mental picture. Moments like this shall live on forever. It's been 88 moving years at Michigan and Trumbull. The tradition built here shall endure along with the permanence of the Old English D. But tonight we must say good-bye. Farewell, old friend Tiger Stadium. We will remember.

TV or Radio?

One of the most frequent questions I get is, "What's the difference between doing radio and TV?" The short answer is simple—you have to wear a tie for one.

On a more serious note, there are several distinctions. With radio, there is much more freedom. You are the eyes and ears for fans. There's an old saying: "It doesn't happen until I say it happens." And in this case, it really is true. If I say a ball is crushed, then it was. This allows the play-by-play guys to have a little more personality. When there's a close play at the plate and we disagree with the call, so do the listeners—they don't know any better.

On television, the pictures do the describing. In fact, while we're watching the game on the field, there are times when we'll quickly focus on the monitor to get a better look at something. Television can really make you look foolish, like if I say a ball is "going, going…" and it dies well short of the wall, the viewer can tell who needs new glasses.

The play-by-play announcer and analyst are really the show on radio. We direct the traffic. If we're going to a sound bite, the producer knows to have it ready to go. If we're going to break, we decide when. It's almost 180 degrees different on television.

That's not to make it seem like we have no input in television. That's far from the truth. Our producers and directors at FOX Sports Detroit are some of the best professionals and people in the business. They are always willing to work with announcers and consider input and opinions.

During 150-plus games, everyone goes through stretches when the ideas run dry, and it's nice to have teammates to pick you up. It truly is a team effort. Sure, there are times when we disagree, which is bound to happen during six long months, but everyone has the same goal—to make the show the best it can be.

Ultimately, though, the producer is responsible for the show. Being the producer is like being the manager. If things go right, the producer's job often goes unnoticed. If things blow up, the producer is the one who gets called into the boss' office the next day.

It takes a team of about 20–25 people on a nightly bases to pull off a telecast. Every single one of them is important. It's no different than a baseball team. You'll have some games that go great, some that go terribly, and then there's the rest of them. There's no chance for success if everyone doesn't pull in the same direction.

It's the same deal in radio, just with a much smaller support staff. Producers, board operators and engineers—that's about the whole team.

Aside from the questions about the difference between radio and TV, the other most frequent question I get is which one do I prefer. After spending the first 15 years in pro baseball as a radio announcer, that is what I was most comfortable with. I really worked hard at the craft and learned the nuances of becoming a good radio play-by-play announcer.

Now a decade into my TV career, I have really come to appreciate the effort it takes on a nightly basis and the creativity required by TV that does not exist as much in radio. It is more of a challenge to do TV, and I have come to embrace that.

But if I am being honest, as Ernie Harwell said, "Baseball is a radio game—always has been and always will be." From a pure play-by-play aspect, I find that to be true.

Rotating Partners

Every now and then you get an opportunity to work with partners other than the one you are normally paired with. For me, I have had a chance to work with several different partners in my career aside from regular partner Rod Allen. Having worked more than a decade in the booth with Rod, we have a good understanding of the other guy's style. When you work with someone else, it can be a good learning experience.

Some of the other analysts I've worked with include Bert Blyleven, Rex Hudler, Al Hrabosky, Jerry Reuss, and Kirk Gibson. They were all major leaguers with varying levels of success, and they all had a unique style and brought their own insight into the game.

We'll start with the Hall of Famer, Bert Blyleven. I've known Bert for years, crossing paths while he was the Minnesota Twins analyst and I was with the Tigers. But in all of those years, we had our first chance to work together in 2011 for a FOX national Tigers-Twins game. On Saturdays, when FOX shows a couple of games to various parts of the nation, they generally try to have both teams represented by the broadcast team.

Anyone who followed Bert as a player knows that he loves two things—baseball and practical jokes. I mean, this is the guy who was the undisputed king of the "hot foot," preying on an unsuspecting player in the dugout by sticking a match in his cleats and lighting it on fire. I may not share much in common with major league players, but I was one of Bert's victims. He got me early in my career, lighting my shoelaces on fire before a game in Anaheim. Suffice it to say that during our first broadcast assignment together, I had one eye on the action and another on my feet.

The game was memorable in that Justin Verlander became a 20-game winner for the first time in his career. Bert uses a nice balance of statistics and analysis to explain the game he loves so much. I was really happy earlier that year when Bert finally made it to the Hall of Fame, in his 14th year of eligibility. He was one hell of a pitcher and is still a hoot.

Then there's Rex Hudler. With a nickname like "Wonder Dog," this guy is definitely a character. Rex was never the most talented player, but through grit and determination he spent 13 years in the big leagues, playing every position except pitcher and catcher.

Both as a player and as a broadcaster, Hudler has always been known for his high-energy delivery and hilarious stories. Need an example? Hud once ate a June bug off his hat on a dare. The Wonder Dog had his snack and collected $800 from his teammates to eat the bug.

Rex is also very quick to turn a phrase. When Tim Salmon would homer for the Angels, it was, "The Kingfish went upstream!" And you'd better swing the bat or you might hear, "You gotta hack or they'll send you back." When we worked together in Anaheim, I had two challenges—staying focused on the game and trying not to burst out laughing.

If you were a baseball fan during the late 1970s and early 1980s, there may not have been a bigger character than Al "The Mad Hungarian" Hrabosky.

As a reliever with the Cardinals, Royals, and Braves, Al would work himself into a frenzy to start an inning and whenever he was at a critical point in the game. Fans who weren't used to seeing his act thought he was having a breakdown.

Three years after he retired, Hrabosky joined the Cardinals broadcasting team and has been there for more than 25 years.

FOX Sports Detroit and FOX Sports Midwest have teamed up a couple of times over the years on Tigers-Cardinals spring-training games. Each team is represented in the booth, which gives fans a different perspective. (It saves money, as well.) The first time Rod and I were teamed up with the Mad Hungarian, I had no idea what to expect.

I can now say that as wild as he was on the field, he's that understated in the booth. This is a guy who obviously knows pitching, and he does a great job of breaking things down for the fans.

Jerry "Rolls" Reuss was twice an All-Star pitcher during his career. He also threw a no-hitter and won 220 games. As strong as he was on the mound, Reuss was always a thoughtful interview with a great yet understated sense of humor.

I worked radio with Jerry Reuss several times in my days in Anaheim. Nobody explained the art of pitching better than Jerry. He'd really make me think beyond the obvious, and he was a blast to work with.

Anyone who watched Kirk Gibson play knew he was a no-nonsense guy who got every drop out of his body. Gibby was my first partner in Detroit. That union lasted only a year before he went back down to the dugout, first as a coach and eventually as the 2011 NL Manager of the Year.

Kirk brought the same intensity into the booth that he showed on the field. He was not afraid to challenge a player's effort on a broadcast. He wasn't looking for confrontation, but just like his days on the field, he wasn't backing down to anyone. As his play-by-play guy, I just stayed out of his way. It may surprise you to know that Gibby, in addition to his feistiness, also had a great ability to use humor as a tool to make his point.

Learning to adapt to the different styles of different partners can be a challenge, but it also makes you grow as a broadcaster. Everyone does it a different way. I look at the relationship between the play-by-play guy and the analyst sort of like the relationship between a pitcher and a catcher. Both guys need each other to make a great team.

WAR, What is it Good For?

The election of 2012 was unforgettable. It featured old school versus new age. The stakes were serious—not just for the two candidates but also for the Midwest and the West Coast. This race would be etched in history and would perhaps set future policy. Oh, I'm not talking about the presidential race between Barack Obama and Mitt Romney. That was important, but I'm referring to the 2012 American League Most Valuable Player Award.

Back in the day, figuring out these awards was at least relatively easy. Voters would look at the core statistics—home runs, batting average and runs batted in for hitters, as well as wins, losses, and earned run average for pitchers.

Over the last 10 years or so, sabermetrics have become a way of life. Now we hear about WAR, ERA+, and WHIP.

The first real sign that award voting was changing occurred in 2009 when Kansas City's Zack Greinke won the American League Cy Young Award with a record of 16–8 despite a trio of guys who were 19-game winners. And it's not like these guys were unknown—Justin Verlander, CC Sabathia, and Felix Hernandez were well-established players.

Greinke's 2.19 ERA was old school, but one of the major factors was his WAR, which stands for wins above replacement. According to this metric, Greinke was worth 10.4 more wins than the average pitcher. None of the 19-game winners had a WAR of more than 6.2.

Fast-forward to 2012, and Tigers fans had no doubt about who should win the Most Valuable Player award in the American League. Miguel Cabrera started strong and never stopped. Every day was like opening a present—what would Miggy do today? In their eyes, it wasn't even close.

Out in Los Angeles, the Angels had made the biggest offseason splash, signing three-time MVP Albert Pujols away from St. Louis. The only problem was that when the season started, Pujols went through the worst slump of his career. As a result, L.A. was nearly out of the playoff chase by the end of April…until they made a move that changed their entire season, and possibly the course of baseball history. They called up minor league phenom Mike Trout.

Almost singlehandedly, the 20-year-old outfielder brought the Angels back into postseason contention with arguably the best rookie season anyone has ever seen.

Despite his late start, Trout hit 30 home runs, led the league in runs and stolen bases, played Gold Glove–caliber defense, and made the All-Star team, all in 139 games. His on-base percentage was nearly .400. Thanks to this incredible rookie, the Angels surged back into the playoff race. He was the unanimous choice as Rookie of the Year. But everyone wondered—could he take home the Most Valuable Player Award?

Meanwhile, Cabrera led his team to its second straight division title. He became the first player since Carl Yastrzemski 45 years earlier to win the

Triple Crown, leading the league in homers, RBI, and batting average. Trout led all of baseball with a WAR of 10.9. Cabrera's WAR was 7.3.

It was truly a case of old school versus new school.

This was a hot debate for the last couple of months of the season. Heading into September, Trout seemed to be the leader. But when Miggy's team needed him the most, he went crazy with 11 home runs and 30 RBI.

True, the Angels won more games than the Tigers, but Cabrera put his team on his back in crunch time. I was actually leaning toward Trout until I witnessed what Cabrera did the final month and a half of the season. Consider these September numbers, with playoff berths on the line:

Trout:	.289 AVG	5 HR	9 RBI	.400 OBP	.900 OPS
Cabrera:	.333 AVG	11 HR	33 RBI	.395 OBP	1.071 OPS

Late in the season as the debate intensified, I polled opposing managers and scouts. Almost universally, the answer was Cabrera. It was hardly a representative sample of the entire league, but it was telling nonetheless. Those managers and scouts made their decisions based on what they saw with their eyes, not a myriad of stats and statistical formulas.

That seemed to give Cabrera a slight edge, but most experts expected a vote for the ages. Personally, I thought Cabrera's consistently great play earned him the MVP. But I don't have a vote, so my opinion really didn't matter.

Trout may very well be the face of baseball's future, and I wouldn't bet against him winning an MVP. But in 2012, there was no denying these stats. Cabrera took home 385 points, while Trout got 282. Case closed.

To me, this was a victory for the old school.

We know how the players felt. In addition to the MVP, Cabrera won the AL Outstanding Player plus the Player of the Year, the latter of which is for both leagues. Those awards are chosen by the players, not the writers. In other words, those guys who competed against Miguel on the field voted him the best player in the game. No stats involved—just respect from peers who compete on a nightly basis against him.

Believe me, I'm not anti-stat. I believe some of the advanced stats are actually quite useful. But it's all about context. Properly used statistics help me do my job, and more importantly, they help the manager do his job. But as we've seen time and time again, the game is played *on* the field. Small-payroll teams beat large-payroll teams. Teams that have no chance can win the World Series. I just don't think you can fit the whole game on a spreadsheet.

Scouts do an incredible amount of work. Most of it is under-appreciated but incredibly valuable. There is certainly something you can learn from driving across the country, watching game after game. I'm not saying that old school is 100 percent right or that the new age is 100 percent wrong. Hey, they may be 50/50. But the really smart teams, like the Tigers, use a little bit of both.

———

People often talk about performance enhancing drugs (PEDs) when it comes to baseball's Hall of Fame, and rightfully so. The legitimacy of the numbers put up by players during the steroid era really presents a dilemma for voters (of which I'm not one). To be able to vote for the Hall of Fame, a person must have served in the Baseball Writers Association of America (BBWAA) for 10 years.

But statistics are also confusing.

It's a shame, too, because as I mentioned, stats can be helpful. But when voting for awards or the Hall of Fame, I think you need to use the eyeball test. Did the player look and feel like a Hall of Famer during his career? Then we can use statistical information to help make the final call. For two examples of this, all you have to do is look at a couple of Tigers legends.

Jack Morris was the winningest pitcher of the 1980s. That's a statistical fact. But who was the winningest pitcher from 1983 to 1993? Nobody knows that answer. I don't think that just because a number ends in zero that it's any different than if it didn't.

If you're of the school that feels Morris belongs in the Hall, you point to the fact that he started 14 Opening Days in a row. That tells you that he was the best pitcher on those pitching staffs. You argue that he was the best pitcher on three world championship teams. (Jack did win a fourth ring, but he was hurt or ineffective for much of that season with Toronto.) You also mention that he pitched perhaps the greatest postseason game, winning Game 7 of the 1991 World Series, by throwing 10 scoreless innings.

Many people have voted against Morris to get to Cooperstown. They look at his 3.90 ERA and his 254 wins (obviously short of the magical 300 total). If you're new age, you point to the fact that he ranks only 145th in WAR. See how confusing this can get?

The other former Tiger great is Alan Trammell. In Detroit, his career is totally appreciated. He led the team to the 1984 World Series (he was the MVP of the Series, as well), made six All-Star teams, and won four Gold Glove Awards. He almost (should have?) won the 1987 MVP Award, and he played all 20 years of his career with the Tigers. His 2,365 hits are actually 25 more than Hall of Famer Barry Larkin. Sounds great, right?

But the naysayers have good points, too. As Tram declined, he only played in more than 100 games twice—and once, it was actually 101 games. While Trammell made those six All-Star squads, Larkin made 12. Defensive metrics show Trammell to be slightly better in the field, but Larkin has an edge at the plate. On the other hand, their WAR is dead even at 91st all-time. So who's worthy?

Just for fun, compare Trammell to the man considered to be perhaps the best shortstop of his era, Ozzie Smith. If you've ever seen a defensive highlight reel, chances are pretty good that "The Wizard" is on it.

Smith played 19 years in the bigs, including 15 All-Star appearances and 13 Gold Gloves. So when you compare Smith and Trammell, it's a no-brainer as to who belongs in the Hall, right?

Not so fast…

While the Wizard made the flashy plays in the field, Tram was more of a blue-collar defender. He got to the most balls and made plays on all of them. In fact, if you look at just raw fielding numbers, Smith made 281 errors in 19 seasons, while Trammell made 227 in 20. Hmm.

Offensively, there's really no comparison. Smith had 195 more hits, but he also had 1,000-plus more at-bats. Trammell's lifetime batting average is .285, while Smith's was .262.

The difference was even more stark in the postseason. Trammell hit .333 in 10 playoff games, winning that World Series MVP and one championship.

Meanwhile, Smith hit .236 with 10 RBI in 42 games, also winning one title.

When each man was eligible for the Hall, however, the numbers were like night and day. Smith coasted in with nearly 92 percent of the vote. (A player needs 75 percent for election). Trammell garnered just less than 16 percent and has slowly gained traction. How can two players who were so similar have such different results?

In my opinion it's because Trammell was more substance over style. This isn't a knock against Smith, but people didn't see Tram on many highlight reels. He didn't make the over-the-shoulder diving plays—he just did his job.

The Hall is littered with cases like these. Voters are damned if they do and damned if they don't.

The Designated Hitter

It was known as the Year of the Pitcher. Bob Gibson set a big-league record in 1968 with an ERA of 1.12, leading the Cardinals to the World Series where they lost to the Tigers, whose pitching staff was anchored by 31-game winner Denny McLain. Nobody has touched either Gibson's or McLain's marks since then. The American League batting champion was Boston's Carl Yastrzemski with an average of .301, the lowest mark in baseball history. After the season, baseball lowered the mound from 15" to 10" high.

While 1968 was the high point (or low point, depending on your perspective), pitching continued to dominate into the early 1970s. In 1973, that changed, at least in the American League.

It is known as Rule 6.10 in the major league rulebook—the Designated Hitter (DH) rule. The junior circuit approved the DH on January 11, 1973, for a three-year trial run.

The Yankees' Ron Blomberg became the first player to appear as a DH on April 6 at Fenway Park. You might say the offense improved immediately. Blomberg worked a bases-loaded walk against Luis Tiant, and the DH was born.

Even now, nearly 40 years after it was born, if you want to start a good argument, ask a few baseball fans whether they like the DH or not.

Because the National League never implemented the DH, baseball is the only sport that has different rules depending on which league you're in. Imagine if the Celtics could shoot three-pointers but the Lakers couldn't, or if the Red Wings had overtimes and shootouts to decide games but the Rangers didn't. That's what the Designated Hitter has done to baseball.

Pitchers bat in the NL, and it makes for a fascinating chess match between managers. If you're trailing 2–0 in the seventh inning, do you pinch hit for the pitcher? It's one reason why bench players in the NL take on a whole new meaning from their American League brethren.

Without the DH, I never would have had the privilege of calling Jim Thome's 600th home run. The likable slugger battled a bad back and hadn't played the field in more than five seasons. Hall of Famer Eddie Murray racked up his 3,000th hit and 500th home run as a DH.

Another Hall of Famer, Paul Molitor, couldn't stay on the field early in his career due to injuries. It's the same for Mariners star Edgar Martinez. And could you imagine the game of baseball without Big Papi? David Ortiz has averaged less than 15 games in the field a year since coming to the Red Sox.

So regardless of how you feel about the DH, love it or hate it, there are arguments on both sides of the fence.

Personally, I prefer the NL style of baseball. I prefer to guess along with the manager, trying to figure out the right move at the right time. But the fact is that the DH isn't going anywhere. The players union would never allow some of their biggest names to lose their jobs.

All of this leaves me almost arguing with myself. I like the no-DH rule, but I can't justify having two different sets of rules. This always seems to be an issue in the World Series and during interleague play.

In 2013, Jim Leyland rolled the dice and put DH Victor Martinez behind the plate in an interleague series against the Mets so that he wouldn't lose his bat in the lineup. Martinez had not caught in a big-league game in two years. Leyland understands the DH's place in the game.

"I think the higher-ups in baseball wanted to see how it would impact the game," he said.

For Leyland, it's not a matter of whether to keep the DH or not, but rather to make it uniform for both leagues.

"It wouldn't make a difference to me which way it went, but I think it should be unified."

I would agree—both leagues should play under the same rules.

Beyond the Numbers

One thing I love about baseball is its numbers. Think about it—if you want to compare your favorite restaurant against another one, how would you do it? You might go by the service or the quality of the food. But that stuff is all subjective.

In baseball, of course, there are subjective measures, but there is also objective data for fans of all levels. Who has more wins? More RBI? Now even those measuring sticks have contributing factors, but you get the picture.

Max Scherzer has improved each season of his career. Some of it can be seen pretty easily. In 2012, he won a career-high 16 games. He was eight behind Justin Verlander for the American League lead in strikeouts. During the second half of the season, Max went 8–2, helping to lead the team to another division title, and he won the clinching game to finish off the Yankees and earn a World Series berth. In 2013, Scherzer became a 20-game winner for the first time in his career. But the most impressive feat I've seen from Max has nothing to do with stats.

In late June 2012, Max's younger brother, Alex, took his own life. Most athletes have a sense of invincibility, and it's easy to see why. They're young, they play the game they love, and they get paid incredible amounts of money to do it. Nothing can stop them. So imagine how difficult it must have been for Max to lose the man he always looked up to—his younger brother.

The Tigers have always been very dedicated to family. GM Dave Dombrowski and manager Jim Leyland both told Max to take as much time as he needed to be with his family. Three days later, Max was on the mound in Pittsburgh, pitching for his team—and for his family—against the Pirates.

The tragedy presented a difficult decision for us to make. We didn't want to ignore the story, yet our job is to present the game every night, and that is usually the main focus. We also didn't want to overstep our bounds because of the nature of Alex's death.

During the broadcast, we decided to stick strictly to baseball. We knew what had happened but tried to respect the Scherzer family's privacy as much as possible. The one thing we had to make sure of was that we didn't sensationalize what had happened.

Max pitched like a man on a mission, striking out seven Pirates in six innings. He lost the game 4–1, but the respect he gained from everyone was immeasurable.

"[It was] the best thing for my family, the best thing for everybody involved. It gave us a chance to get out of the house. It was a chance to put a smile on everyone's face," Scherzer told the *Detroit News*. "For me to go out there that day was pretty special for my family. I said I would do it only if my whole family could be there. But I won't lie. It was a lot harder than I thought."

Athletes perform with adversity every day. So do accountants, teachers, and everyone else. We've all been touched by death in one way, shape, or form.

Baseball is a difficult game to master mentally. It had to be hard enough for Scherzer to deal with the death of his brother to begin with, but because Alex took his own life, the physiological pain for Max had to be that much more difficult.

For Max to put that aside and compete in a major league game so soon after his brother's death left me speechless.

Postseason Randomness

There's a feeling in baseball that legends are born in the postseason, and it's not necessarily star players who always rise to the occasion on the big stage.

Some of baseball's all-time greats failed in the playoffs. Ted Williams is often considered the best hitter who ever lived. In his one World Series, the Splendid Splinter hit .200. In his first five playoff appearances, Barry Bonds never hit better than .261. For every Mr. October (Reggie Jackson), there have been several good-to-great players who couldn't break through.

On the other hand, who could have imagined that guys like Rick Dempsey, Scott Brosius, or Ray Knight would lead their teams to championships? These guys were all solid players, but by getting hot at the right time, they became October legends. Of course, the least likely postseason hero of all was Brian Doyle in 1978.

Doyle wasn't even the best second baseman in his own family—that honor would belong to his brother, Denny, who was an average player during his eight-year career. Brian never even played 40 games in any one season, and his lifetime batting average was a whopping .161. But he got the opportunity of a lifetime in 1978 when All-Star second baseman Willie Randolph pulled his hamstring. The world champions needed some help.

Insert Doyle, who had only appeared in 39 games. During the ALCS victory over Kansas City, Doyle played three games and went 2–7. But he was just warming up. Doyle took advantage of the stage, hitting .438 as the Yankees defeated the Dodgers in six hard fought games. Another unlikely hero, Bucky Dent, took home MVP honors.

In 2006, the Tigers were victims of some unlikely postseason heroics. That squad came out of nowhere to lead the Central Division for nearly the entire season. They faltered down the stretch but secured a Wild Card playoff spot. After knocking off the Yankees in the Division Series and sweeping Oakland out of the ALCS, Jim Leyland's team was a heavy favorite to win the World Series. St. Louis had the worst record of any playoff team that year and needed seven hard-fought games to defeat the Mets in the NLCS.

Game 1 of the World Series looked like a mismatch. Rookie of the Year Justin Verlander had won 17 games for Detroit. The Cardinals answered with Anthony Reyes, who was 5–8 with an ERA of more than five. The Tigers figured to roll through this game and be on their way to a championship.

Unfortunately, someone forgot to tell Reyes. Verlander got shelled while Reyes threw eight innings of four-hit, two-run ball. The Cardinals took Game 1 en route to a five-game Series win.

The tables were turned a bit in 2012. The big, bad New York Yankees won

95 games, seven more than the Tigers. I felt like Detroit was the better team, but New York had its typical star-studded lineup, including guys like Jeter, A-Rod, Cano, and Granderson. But October can be fickle.

The Tigers swept the Yankees without much trouble. Yes, they caught a break in the first game when Jeter broke his ankle, but the numbers really do tell the story.

Robinson Cano is considered one of the two or three best hitters in the game. He came into the playoffs with hits in 24 of his last 39 at-bats. And when Cano gets going, you simply cannot throw the ball past him.

Maybe we should have seen it coming. Cano was just 2–22 against the Orioles in the first round. But when you talk about a talent like his, you had to figure he'd bust out against Detroit. Well, he busted. There is no way you can explain what happened to Cano against the Tigers. As Yankees broadcaster John Sterling might say, "Cano…Cannot."

In 18 at-bats, he had one hit. The Gold Glove–winner also struggled defensively, but it was his hitting, or lack thereof, that helped change the series.

Cano had company, though, and in a big way. Former Tiger Curtis Granderson smashed 43 home runs during the season, just one behind Miguel Cabrera for the major league lead. He had always had some dramatic moments against his old team…but not this year. Grandy was hitless in 11 at-bats, with seven strikeouts and two walks. He was yanked from the starting lineup in Game 4—not what the team needed.

Nick Swisher belted 24 home runs during the regular season but was 3–12 with a single RBI. Eric Chavez, a regular-season revelation with 16 homers, went 0–8 with four strikeouts.

But the worst, most staggering performance was by the highest-paid player in all of baseball. Alex Rodriguez was huge in the Yankees championship run of 2009 but has generally struggled in the playoffs. Yet 2012 was actually historic.

First came the 2–16 performance against the Orioles in the first round. But that was just an appetizer. Next up was a series against the Tigers. A-Rod's history in Detroit was not what you'd call terrific. In the 2006 playoffs, Joe Torre infamously dropped Rodriguez to eighth in the batting order, but 2012 made that look like nothing.

After Rodriguez went 1–7 in the first two games, Yankees manager Joe Girardi actually benched A-Rod in Game 3, which ended up as another Tigers win. Then, with his team facing elimination, Alex was on the bench again. I can't recall this ever happening in any other sport.

Rodriguez came in to pinch hit during Game 4 and made two soft outs. In fairness, he was battling hip problems that became more obvious after the series, but this was another colossal postseason failure for one of the most prolific players in baseball history.

After beating the Yankees, the Tigers were again favored to beat San Francisco in the World Series. Because of a tough NLCS, the Giants were forced to start Barry Zito in Game 1 against Verlander. Zito was such an afterthought that he wasn't even on San Francisco's roster the last time they won the title. Verlander was the defending Cy Young and MVP winner. Sure enough, Pablo Sandoval hit three home runs, and the Giants were on their way.

JV wasn't the only Tiger star to struggle. Triple Crown winner Miguel Cabrera and fellow slugger Prince Fielder combined to go 4–27, and the Tigers were swept in four games.

Just when you think you've got it figured out, postseason baseball will teach you how little you actually know.

A New Season

As much as we all live for the postseason, there's nothing like the excitement of spring training. Part of it is physical—traveling to Lakeland, Florida, for some sun (hopefully) after a few months of another rugged Midwest winter. But a huge part of the attraction is emotional—the sense of renewal as everyone gets ready for another marathon known as the baseball season. Players hone their timing and round into shape. The coaching staff maps out a game plan for the upcoming 162 games. And yes, broadcasters and writers research their storylines to share with our audience.

There are certain simple sights that never get old. I love watching fathers taking their sons and daughters to the ballpark and scoring autograph after autograph from their sports heroes. Everybody has time and is in a relaxed state of mind.

For me, it's like a family reunion, walking into the clubhouse for the first time, greeting players, coaches, and the manager. It's an annual rite of spring, answering the annual "How was your winter?" question as you get reacquainted with the folks who will become your second family for the next six months.

I love visiting with the ushers and vendors that I've come to know over the years. We only see most of these folks for a couple of months, but when we return each year, it's like we never left.

Players love spring training because everything is intense and laid back at the same time. Yes, they're there to work and prepare for their jobs. Even while there are games every day, players only play for a few innings, then they go do extra work, play golf, or spend time with their families.

I miss my family when they're not there, but I love either taking a walk or run around Lake Hollingsworth every morning before heading to the ballpark, where I'll stick around for most of the game.

Coming back year after year, you learn the inside secrets around Joker Marchant Stadium. One of my favorites is the story of Ty Cobb and Jim Leyland.

Inside the manager's office, there is a photo of the Georgia Peach. Thirty years ago, when Leyland was the manager of the Class A Lakeland Tigers, he was so frustrated after a tough loss that he threw his spikes at the wall. In a cruel twist of irony, the spikes punctured a hole in the photo of Cobb, who was known for spiking opponents. Now, all these years later, the photo is still there, and so is the hole. I guess what goes around comes around, even for the greatest Tiger of them all.

Decade after decade, families have planned their winter vacations around spring training. You can feel the buzz when the Tigers have a chance to be really good. The enthusiasm permeates the fan base in a tangible way…sometimes more tangible than others.

Every year you'll see kids running around, trying to get foul balls. I saw one young man who paid the price but ended up with the prize. Between two of the practice fields is a nice little alley for everyone to stretch out, watch what's going on, and get autographs. One day, Tigers coach Glenn Ezell smoked a foul ball that ripped right down the alley. A seven-year-old boy tried to get his hands up, but the ball smacked him right in the chest. The ball ricocheted against a fence where a bunch of fans scrambled to retrieve it.

The child's concerned father ran over to him and looked at a shocking baseball-size bruise on his son's chest.

"Are you okay?" the father asked.

The boy struggled to catch his breath. "Dad, it hurt…but I got the ball!"

That sums up spring training. As excited as he was to snag a (painful) souvenir, I could relate.

Back in my first spring training in 2002, nothing put me more at ease than Ernie Harwell asking me out to lunch.

"I know this great little Italian place up the road," Ernie said.

"Great. I'd love to join you," I said. I was eager to test out the local restaurants, and to do it with Ernie was a dream scenario. Ten minutes later, we pulled into the Olive Garden. I could only laugh.

It taught me a lesson I'll never forget, though. Spring training is for kids of all ages…even middle-aged men.

I've Got to Be Me

It's the most exciting play in sports, and it can also be the most thrilling experience for a broadcaster. It is the home run.

Dramatic home runs are something fans never forget. When you hear a classic home run call, you instantly remember where you were when it happened. Think about it:

"I don't believe what I just saw!"
—Jack Buck describing Kirk Gibson's pinch hit homer off of
Dennis Eckersley in Game 1 of the 1988 World Series.

"Touch 'em all, Joe. You'll never hit a bigger home run in your life!"
—Tom Cheek's call of Joe Carter's walk-off home run to
wrap up the 1993 World Series.

165

"The Giants win the pennant! The Giants win the pennant! The Giants win the pennant!"

—Russ Hodges' iconic call of Bobby Thomson's Shot Heard 'Round the World in 1951.

In many ways a baseball announcer's main calling card is his home-run call. Say the right thing at the right time, and you'll have a place in history. So, of course, there is an element of luck. The great Ernie Harwell was broadcasting that Giants classic in 1951 on television. Unfortunately, most of us have never heard Ernie's call because the tapes got destroyed.

Each of these calls have one thing in common—they all captured the drama of the moment and were all unscripted. I often get asked, "What would you say if you were calling Game 7 of the World Series and Miguel Cabrera hit the game-winning home run?" My answer is always the same. I wouldn't know until it happened.

Some announcers have a standard home-run call. You've probably heard them:

"It is high. It is far. It is gone!"

—John Sterling of the Yankees.

"You can put it on the board…yes!"

—Ken "Hawk" Harrelson with the White Sox.

"Get up, baby. Get up. Yeah!"

—Mike Shannon for the Cardinals.

That's their choice. They've all had successful careers doing their own thing. But for me, I've never felt that one home-run call fits all sizes. That's why I have never had a single home-run call. Just like all home runs are different—not every one is high, far, and gone—I think all calls should be different, as well. My philosophy is call what I see, and just let it happen.

It's funny because as kids, we all pretended we were calling games, and we probably had 10 scripted calls ready to go. "Broadcasting" in the basement is one thing…doing it for real is something else.

Talk to ten different people, and you'll get ten different answers about what the play-by-play man should say during an exciting moment.

When I was a young announcer for the Angels in the mid-1990s, the club's newly hired broadcast manager called me into his office one day to share his thoughts with me. He suggested that I create a home-run call. He felt I needed to raise my level of excitement to take my career to the "next level."

His intentions were well-founded, but he didn't realize that all announcers have different skills. One thing I've learned over the years is that when you're on-camera, you have to be who you are. Viewers can sniff out a phony in a minute.

I've always tried to be coachable throughout my career, so against my better judgment, I gave his method a shot. So for the next three weeks I made an effort to inject extra excitement into every home run and create a home-run call.

Since I'm Italian, one of my buddies in California suggested I should be a smart ass and end my home-run call with, "Now that's a spicy meata-balla!"

No thanks.

The problem was, I began to call routine pop-ups as deep fly balls. It all sounded so forced that even I wouldn't have watched me. I sounded like a guy on *Saturday Night Live* trying to be Joe Sportscaster. It didn't take long for me to realize that you can't script the way you call games, and that includes a home-run call.

That's not to say others haven't been able to pull it off. It's just not my style. I think a great home-run call is unique, genuine, and captures the emotion of that moment. In my opinion, you just can't do that if it's scripted.

The Real Heroes

People often ask me what the best and worst part of my job is, and my response is always the travel. It's not a lot of fun flying home from Oakland on a Sunday night after a 10-game West Coast swing. Yes, we're flying on a charter with every possible amenity, but it's still not easy. Once in a while, however, you go on a trip that changes your life.

When I'm not broadcasting for the Tigers, I have spent the winter months calling Oakland University basketball games. I enjoy staying busy, but truth be told, by the end of hoops season, I'm usually pretty spent. I take spring training to catch my breath and get ready for the baseball season.

Even during Oakland's season, I try to do Tigers-related community appearances, such as Tigerfest and things like that. But what I did in February 2013 was the chance of a lifetime.

That was when FOX Sports Detroit general manager Greg Hammaren asked me if I'd like to represent our region on a trip to Germany to visit our troops.

"Germany? Like the real Germany?" I asked.

"Yes, Germany."

"There's not like a Germany, Ohio, or anything, right?"

"No, the one in Europe."

While I don't have any direct ties to the military, I've always felt like we should always do whatever we can to support our troops both at home and abroad. Each season, I package the Tigers Home Opener onto a DVD and make it available to our brave men and women so they can enjoy some baseball while they serve abroad.

It's a labor of love, an idea I hatched with our late public relations manager, Tim Bryant. Even after Tim's death, it's something that I want to do for the troops and to honor Tim.

So the opportunity to bring spring training to the troops in Grafenwoehr, Germany, was really a no-brainer.

We had a pretty cool crew that headed out. I joined Hall of Famers Rollie Fingers and Wade Boggs, along with current players Heath Bell and Luke Gregerson and former stars Bob Brenly, Tim Salmon, and David Justice on a trip to the U.S. Army Garrison in Grafenwoehr. We were also joined by FOX Sports Girls from various regions, including Detroit. Our mission was to spend some time with our troops and bring baseball to them. The plan was that just a few hours mixing with the soldiers would allow them to forget about being away from their loved ones. Little did we know that it would be the troops who would make the visit special for us.

We spent three exhilarating days on the army base, taking part in clinics, military exercises, and school visits. It was pretty hectic, but really special, too. The second day of the trip was the most intense. We were to meet a group of troops and participate in their morning exercise training.

At 5:30 AM, I dragged my jet-lagged body out of a warm bed and stumbled downstairs where Boggs, Salmon, Brenly, Fingers, and Justice were fully awake and already waiting. Show-offs. I *know* those guys weren't up at 5:30 during their playing days…

After a five-minute bus ride to the exercise area of the Garrison, it was time to fall in with a group of soldiers who looked like they were salivating at the thought of getting their hands on a load of out-of-shape civilians. We hadn't really been told of the day's itinerary, but we were about to find out.

We were informed that we would participate in an exercise circuit program that would feature running, push-ups, stretching, and various other calisthenics. My inner voice told me that this wasn't going to end well. Maybe it was because it was 20 degrees out. Maybe it was because we were all out late the night before. Or maybe it was because, well, we're old.

Still, the chance to train with some of the county's soldiers was an experience I won't ever forget.

We were also given an opportunity to experience some of the virtual training our troops engage in. With a video screen in front of me, I was selected to be the gunner. I listened as our commander barked out orders over a headset. The exercise simulated being part of a convoy in enemy territory. The results were alarming. We ran into a tree, and I took out only one insurgent, pretty much putting our vehicle in peril for the entire exercise. If only my son were there, he would have wiped out the enemy with his advanced video-game skills. Even this simulation gave me a sense of the pressure these soldiers deal with every day. This is a job where you can't have an off day.

Day 3 was just as packed as the Days 1 and 2. We made a stop at a transitional facility designed to help our injured troops assimilate back into society or return to active duty. We took a ride in an armored fighting vehicle called a Stryker, and a visit to the 2nd Cavalry Regiment Reed Museum highlighted the day. It was like taking a journey through the lives of some great Americans. This was also a great chance to really talk with these heroic men and women. We learned that every soldier has his or her own story.

There was a young man from Texas who was constantly getting in trouble with the law and wanted to set a better example for his young brother, so he enlisted. Mission accomplished. I spoke with a retired military father who didn't want his son to enlist because he didn't want his boy to see the things he saw in combat. His son enlisted anyway, and now this dad could not be more proud.

And it wasn't just men. We spoke with a young woman who loves the Tigers. She suffered back and eye injuries in combat and was in a facility designed to transition her back into society. Having served her country, all she wanted was to get married and start a family. I know she'll be a great wife and mother.

As the trip came to a close, it was difficult to leave the people we had become friends with. It was only three days, but we knew people's names, their stories, and vice versa. If we felt like this after three days, I can only imagine the bond these soldiers feel amongst themselves, spending every day in high-pressure situations.

Another cool aspect of this trip was spending time with the ballplayers. I knew Salmon pretty well from my Angels days, but hanging out with Boggs, Brenly, Fingers, and the group was great. A trip like this shows that it doesn't matter if you're in the Hall of Fame or if you've won a World Series as a player or a manager. On this trip, we were all honored to be visitors of the heartbeat of our country.

I think our entire group was thankful for the opportunity to get a glimpse of what military life is like overseas. FOX Sports can be proud of the initiative. Our troops constantly reminded us how much they appreciated what we did for them.

The truth is, what they do for us is far more important.

The Big Time

When I talk to high school or college kids about their future careers, I often use the saying, "Find the top rung of your ladder." In other words, as you prepare for your career, identify what your dream job would be and strive for it.

One thing I've learned is that your dream job may be different than mine. That doesn't make either of us right, and it doesn't make anyone wrong. Everyone has different personalities and goals.

For many young broadcasters, the dream is to land a network job. It could be working for MLB Network or calling a Super Bowl for FOX. When I decided to get into the business, I had two distinct goals—become a big-league broadcaster, and do it in my hometown of Detroit.

Detroit has a rich history of broadcasting talent across all of the major sports. Bruce Martyn was the voice of the Red Wings in my youth, and George Blaha was the voice of the Pistons. Both were great announcers that became synonymous with their respective teams and the city of Detroit. For the Tigers, Ernie Harwell, Paul Carey, and George Kell were the voices of summer. All three men forged a special relationship with the fans of Detroit.

There is a special bond that announcers have with the cities in which they work. That is one advantage that national announcers do not have. Working at FOX Sports Detroit has given me the opportunity to work some games for FOX Sports on its *Game of the Week* telecasts over the past few years.

It's a great honor, and we get to work with some of the most talented people in the business, just as I get to in my "day job." Yet as special as those games are, there are challenges, as well.

There is a rhythm you develop when you work with your local crew during the season. Your producers and directors know your style and vice versa. The promos are the same every night, and you develop a relationship with your stage manager. That is not the case with national telecasts.

The national production crew works together every week, but with different announcers. It's that way for the producer, director, and technical folks, but it's also a new dynamic in the booth.

My first national chance came in 2011 when I was paired with Twins analyst and Hall of Famer Bert Blyleven. I've known Bert for a long time and was glad to hear I would be working with him.

Before the game I chatted with Bert, and he said he was excited to work with me. In Bert language, that means he was looking forward to lighting my shoes on fire. Blyleven's curveball was regarded as one of the greatest in baseball history, but his reputation as the king of the hot foot is indisputable.

Being a starting pitcher, Bert had a great deal of free time, and he wasn't afraid to use it. He'd sneak up on a teammate and light his shoelaces on fire. It never failed to get a laugh. I was semi-honored when he tried to hotfoot me in the mid-1990s.

Our first game together was a Tiger-Twins matchup. Justin Verlander was on the hill, looking for the first 20-win season of his career. JV didn't have his best stuff, giving up four runs in six innings, but it was enough to get No. 20. I remember thinking how cool it was to be working a game featuring a potential Hall of Famer and broadcasting it with a Hall of Famer.

The next year, I had another chance to work for FOX. This time, I was paired with *Sports Illustrated* columnist and MLB Network announcer Tom Verducci while the Tigers hooked up with the Indians in Cleveland. This time I got an up-close look at the main difference between doing a national broadcast and a local telecast. When you do a national game, you have to play it much more down the middle. No matter how fair you are to both teams, each set of fans will always maintain that you are favoring the other team.

Turner's Ernie Johnson probably put it best while covering the 2012 ALCS between the Tigers and Yankees, saying, "I've gotten 50 emails from Tigers fans complaining that I am favoring the Yankees and 50 emails from Yankees fan complaining that I am favoring the Tigers."

That goes with the territory, but on this national broadcast, it was the Tigers fans who wanted my head on a platter. Tigers starter Anibal Sanchez was throwing a no-hitter through six innings.

Normally I won't actually use the term "no-hitter" on our home broadcast because of baseball etiquette. (You can look it up—I didn't use it in either of Verlander's no-no's or in Armando Galarraga's "imperfect" game.) On this day, though, since it was a national telecast, our producer was busy digging up statistics to support a possible no-hitter.

During the commercial break before the bottom of the seventh, our producer Carol Langley informed me that we would have a graphic about no-hitters in Tigers history. Since this was a national telecast, I had no choice but to talk about it and use the term "no-hitter."

My only hope was that Sanchez would throw the no-hitter and save me from "jinxing" it.

Sanchez retired the first two Indians in the bottom of the seventh before Carlos Santana tripled off the center-field wall to end the drama. And there it was, as far as some Tigers fans were concerned—I ended the no-hitter by talking about it.

After the game, my phone was blowing up. My buddies back home were texting me that I was getting killed on the local sports talk station for "ruining" the no-hitter.

National telecasts are a tremendous experience, and I am always grateful for the opportunity to do them, but doing Tigers baseball is still the top rung of my ladder. It is what I have always strived for, and I don't need the notoriety of the national scene to define my career.

Support, Not Illumination

Musician Edwin Starr asked the question in 1970. "War, what is it good for?" Today's scouts and veteran talent evaluators wouldn't hesitate to answer, "Absolutely nothing."

"War" in Starr's era meant something totally different than the WAR of today's baseball world. WAR stands for wins above replacement.

The war (pun intended) between front-office folks who favor new-age stats and traditional scouts is intensifying by the year. If I had to park myself in one of the camps, I would lean toward old school.

I am not anti-statistics by any means. Some of the newer advanced stats can be valuable in evaluating talent or telling a story. I think there is room for everyone.

But that doesn't mean I'm totally ready to dive in. First, I'm terrible at math, and trying to decipher how some of these stats are calculated gives me a headache. Second, I'm borderline ADD, and there's no shot I'll take the time to understand every stat. That doesn't mean I don't think they are interesting.

I am often asked when we will take our broadcasts out of the stone age and start to incorporate stats such as WAR, DIPS (defense-independent pitching statistics), ERA+ and VORP (value over replacement player) into the broadcast. The answer is probably not anytime soon.

There are a few problems. In general, TV can use too many stats. Like I said, if they tell a story, then great. But I'm not a fan of bogging down a broadcast with excessive stats. The second problem is that viewers want to be able to enjoy the game. Yes, baseball is a thinking man's game, but nobody wants to think that hard. The broadcast would be so slow it would ruin the flow of the game.

I don't mind using stats like WHIP. It is relatively east to explain—walks plus hits per innings pitched. An audience can grasp that quickly. But if it takes more than a pitch or two to explain, people have a tendency to tune you out.

Vin Scully had a wonderful line about statistics. Scully once said, "Statistics are used much like a drunk uses a lamppost—for support, not illumination."

If you prefer your explanations a bit more coarse, former NFL coach Buddy Ryan said this: "Statistics are like loose women—you can make them do whatever you want."

I'll leave the wise old sayings to others and the advanced stats to the sabermetricians. "The simpler the better" is a valuable motto in broadcasting.

This Is Going to Be a Long Day

Practice doesn't always make perfect. Pitchers often talk about how they can't judge what kind of day they will have by how they are throwing in the bullpen as they warm up for a start.

The curve might be sharp, the fastball crisp, and all signs point are pointing to a good day, yet when they take the mound, nothing feels right...or vice versa.

The same goes for announcers. The words might be flowing during rehearsal, and you may feel like you are locked in with your ideas, but when the red light goes on, sometimes nothing comes out right.

Just like the athletes we cover on a daily basis, we suffer from the same fatigue, both mentally and physically, that they do. In fairness, the players' physical issues are usually a little more serious than ours. I haven't missed a game yet due to a strained oblique.

But in all seriousness, the rigors of the major league schedule can have a tremendous effect on how your mind processes situations on the field and how you ultimately describe them. In that way, it's probably like working at a bank or post office—there are times when we all get a little bleary-eyed.

Every announcer, regardless of sport and experience level, has experienced this. You see the play develop in front of you and, for some reason, the words just won't come out in the proper order.

I've had my share of bloopers, and I'm sure there are more to come.

One year while I was broadcasting in Anaheim, the Angels were letting a big lead slip away in the ninth inning. The Halos closer, Troy Percival, began warming up in the bullpen. It was a long night, and as the Angels were coughing it up, I tried to say, "It looks like Troy Percival is up and throwing in the Angels pen." What I actually said was, "It looks like Troy Percival is throwing up in the Angels pen," which technically would probably have described how Percival was feeling about his team's performance that night.

There is always the old standby—the accidental swear word—that finds its way on the air. One night as I was discussing the best third baseman to ever play the game, I was making a case for Mike Schmidt. Except I didn't say Schmidt. I said something that rhymes with Schmidt. I'm guessing you know what I mean.

I was broadcasting professional hockey for the Peoria (Illinois) Rivermen of the International Hockey League in 1987. The Rivermen had a fast, shifty scorer named Ron Handy. Handy was always the top target of the opposing team's goon. One night in Fort Wayne, Indiana, Handy was slithering his way through the Fort Wayne defense when he was suddenly upended at center ice by a defender.

My description of the hit is one I will never forget. I meant to say, "Handy was dumped at center ice." Instead, for reasons I still can't understand, I uttered the words, "Handy took a dump at center ice." The old switchboard was lighting up back at the station after that one.

Male genitalia humor is always good for an embarrassing gaffe. I was broadcasting in Davenport, Iowa, in the summer of 1989. One night, a ground ball was hit back to the pitcher with the winning run at third and two outs. The ball got stuck in the webbing of the pitcher's glove. As he desperately tried to dislodge the ball and throw the runner out, he just couldn't get the ball loose and the winning run scored. My description was as follows: "Hit sharply back to Rodriguez. The ball is stuck in the webbing of his glove, and the winning run will score with no throw. And Rodriguez is left standing there, holding his balls with his glove."

Mental fatigue goes beyond bloopers. There are times when I will see a play clearly in my mind, but for some inexplicable reason, it just doesn't come out right. For example, I could actually see the ball hit to Miguel Cabrera, but I couldn't remember his name.

"Ground ball to third…fielded by…you know…the MVP and Triple Crown winner…yeah, that guy…the guy whose name I call thousands of times a year. He fires to first for the out."

The mind can be a spooky thing. Or sometimes it's as simple as the audio mix in your headset is just not right.

The longer you do this, the more you learn that you will never be perfect. Some nights you just can't get it right. The words get tangled, and it can be a helpless feeling to know that you have 8½ more innings of play-by-play to call.

It's like the guy who goes 0–4. It's going to happen, so you just try to limit the clunkers.

The Love of the Game

Broadcasting Major League Baseball is the greatest job in the world. Okay, let me amend that—aside from being a major league player, broadcasting Major League Baseball is the greatest job in the world. I mean, think about it.

Our office has a view of the field! It's kind of tough to complain about much.

We also get paid to watch the best players in the world on a nightly basis. It makes you feel really fortunate that someone decided you were worthy of a press credential.

The downside of doing what we do is that in some ways you become anesthetized to how fortunate you are to be there. I always keep in mind that so many people only get to one or two games a year. Something as simple as a Miguel Cabrera RBI single may be routine for us, but for those fans, it's the thrill of a season.

I remember as a kid following the Tigers and how much I lived and died with each game. One game has stuck with me through the years. It was 1975, and the Tigers were at Shea Stadium. Our first baseman, Nate Colbert, hit a grand slam off Pat Dobson late in the game, and the Tigers beat the Yanks 7–2. I remember the feeling of pure excitement.

The Tigers would go on to lose 102 games that year, and Colbert's grand slam was just a footnote in a miserable season, but it didn't matter to me. I loved my team, and I would live and die with them through thick and thin.

I see that same passion in Tigers fans today. Fortunately, fans now have more information and access than ever before. Every game is on TV, and we know more of the details about every player. Access and information allow fans to be better connected with their heroes. Every game and every pitch are dissected through Twitter, Facebook, and everything else. Win or lose, fans care as much as ever, and these days they have the platforms to share their thoughts.

Being a broadcaster has taught me about staying on an even keel. When you watch every game, you realize that the game is not nearly as easy as it looks on TV.

We've all heard the adage that the season is a marathon, not a sprint. Don't get too up when the team wins, and don't get too low when it loses. It's pretty common sense stuff.

That is, unless I'm at home watching the game when it's a national broadcast.

I immediately turn into a lunatic, screaming and yelling at the screen with every twist and turn of the game. It's like I don't understand how these guys

Willie Horton (right) is congratulated by Gary Sutherland (left) also of the Tigers and Nate Colbert (center) while crossing home plate after hitting a homer in the top of the sixth inning in a game against the New York Yankees in New York, Friday, April 11, 1975. The Tigers won the game 5–3. *(AP Photo/Dave Pickoff)*

can't get every clutch hit. It's those days that make me realize how much working in the game can sometimes rob your passion for the sport.

Broadcasting a game is much different than sitting on your couch watching it. I've found that the pressures of broadcasting on live television make you concentrate so much on you duties that you lose the passion a fan would have. If Rod and I were to jump up and down every time the Tigers got a big hit or slammed down our headsets at every error, we'd never be able to do our job.

That's the downside of being around the sport every single day. It becomes a test of endurance to get through the season. To be totally truthful, some nights the only stat you are interested in is time of game.

After all these years in the game, sometimes I question whether I'll ever have that passion from when Nate Colbert hit that grand slam. Not knowing that answer can be depressing.

But all it takes is watching some games while sitting on the couch, or being in the stands during the playoffs, and I snap right back to reality.

That is reassuring because, after all, this is a kid's game, and there will always be some kid inside of me.

A Spooky Home-Field Advantage

One of the toughest trips for American League teams is when they travel to Tampa. The Rays have made an incredible transformation from laughingstock into perennial power.

Despite Joe Maddon's exciting brand of baseball, playing at Tropicana Field can be downright depressing. "The Trop" is dank, usually half-empty, and lacking atmosphere. You might say it's like watching a game in a mausoleum.

In television, we call this a segue.

For a broadcast team, Tampa is a great place to visit. Of course, the obvious perk is the weather. That really doesn't need any explanation. But when you travel as much as we do, the accommodations can often define a trip.

All hotels in the big leagues are great—that's why it's the big leagues. We are fortunate to stay in the best places, and we get treated like royalty. Still, some hotels stand out more than others.

The Vinoy in St. Petersburg is one of those hotels. This place has it all. Its pool is always heavily populated, and the view of the bay is breathtaking. Oh yeah, there are also ghosts.

Maybe I should explain.

The Vinoy dates back to the mid-1920s and housed famous guests like Babe Ruth and actor Jimmy Stewart. The cavalcade of stars continued in the 1950s and 1960s, with names like Marilyn Monroe and Joe DiMaggio filling out the guestbook. During WWII, the Vinoy shut down as a hotel and was leased to the U.S. Army Air Force and used as a training center. In 1944, the Vinoy reopened up its doors to the public, and a year later it was purchased by Chicago businessman Charles H. Alberding for $700,000.

The hotel suffered a slow decline during the 1950s and 1960s. By the early 1970s, the once-glorious resort had turned into a low-income boarding house. Where nightly rates had been in the hundreds of dollars, "guests" were now paying $7 a night. Eventually, the doors were closed for good.

But in 1992, the property opened once again, and by the middle of the decade, the Vinoy was back as a prestigious resort. Every team loves staying there.

And there are the ghosts.

It's not like the entire hotel is haunted—just room 521. The stories are endless, with the most popular being about a woman who was allegedly murdered in the room and still roams the fifth floor.

Before you roll your eyes, consider this: water faucets turn on by themselves; doors open and close mysteriously; lights flicker in the rooms. All of these actions are supposedly the results of spirits floating through the Vinoy.

And it's not like this comes from one source, either. Former Reds reliever Scott Williamson swears to this day that he saw a man in his room and that while he was sleeping, he felt someone pushing down on his chest.

Every team seems to have a story. I never thought Prince Fielder would ever meet his match. I mean, Prince is not the type of guy you'd expect to be afraid of ghosts. He's a pretty big dude, one who usually does the scaring himself. But during the 2012 season, the Tigers had just finished a series in Texas and we arrived at the Vinoy in the early morning hours. Everyone was exhausted.

Players, coaches, trainers, and broadcasters shuffled through the lobby, grabbing room keys and looking forward to a good night's sleep. But Prince had a nightmare before even hitting the elevator button. His room was on the "haunted" fifth floor.

While almost everyone else was headed to their rooms, Prince had a look of defiance on his face. "Uh, no way," he said. "That floor is haunted. I need another room on another floor."

Initially, I thought he was kidding. "Are you serious?" I asked.

"I don't take any chances," he replied.

With that, Prince was moved to a "non-haunted" floor and I was left thinking that if a guy the size of Prince is intimidated, I should probably sleep with my eyes open.

Oh, and Prince went 3–15 in the series.

Closing Time

On the surface, it seems simple. Get three outs, sometimes with a three-run cushion, shake some hands, and walk back to the clubhouse. For the truly elite closers, it is that simple…most of the time.

The role of the closer is one of the biggest changes in baseball during the last 40 years. Back in the 1970s, guys like Rollie Fingers, Mike Marshall, and Rich "Goose" Gossage would frequently come into the game in the seventh inning with men on base, get out of the jam, and finish off the game. They were called "firemen" because they were always called on to put out the fire. But in the mid-1980s, Tony La Russa started what became a seismic shift in managerial strategy.

La Russa and the Oakland A's acquired Dennis Eckersley from the Chicago Cubs. On the surface, it seemed like a nothing move. "Eck" was on the downside of his career. He had thrown a no-hitter in Cleveland, won 20 games in Boston, but also dealt with a drinking problem and was 6–11 with a 4.57 ERA in his last year in the Windy City. Oakland gave up three players who never reached the majors to acquire Eckersley.

La Russa decided to try Eckerlsey in the bullpen. But he wouldn't be the prototypical closer. Eck was going to become a specialist—he would only pitch the ninth inning, most of the time starting the inning with nobody on base. Oh, and it had to be a save situation. During his time in Oakland, Eck would only pitch in non-save spots about 10 times per year.

The A's of the 1980s were all about specialization. Left-handed pitcher Rick Honeycutt would only come into face left-handers; *this* guy would pitch to *those* guys. Bullpens would never be the same.

The Red Sox bought into baseball sabermetric guru Bill James' theory that your "closer" should pitch whenever the biggest spot in the game occurred, whether it was two men on in the seventh inning or bases loaded in the eighth. The idea was not about saves but a type of throwback to the 1970s. That theory was a huge failure in Boston, and today teams only really use the closer for the last three outs.

Closers today have a completely different job than their pre-Eckersley counterparts. Mariano Rivera is considered the greatest closer of all time, and while he has gone more than one inning (usually in the playoffs), he generally has the same workload as everyone else.

The best closers in the game have a save conversion rate of roughly 90–94 percent. If that sounds like a high percentage with little room for error, it should. Any team that is even thinking about contending needs to have at the least a very good closer.

Every once in a while, the stars align perfectly. In 2008, Brad Lidge was a perfect 41–41 in save opportunities. No wonder he was on the mound for the last out as the Phillies beat the Rays for their first World Series title in 28 years.

After the 2009 season, the Tigers were in the market for a closer. The team's all-time saves leader, Todd Jones, had retired, and while Jim Leyland is one of the best bullpen mixers and matchers in the game, everyone likes to have "the guy." So GM Dave Dombrowski went out and got arguably the best closer on the market, Jose Valverde.

"Papa Grande" was not what you'd call a shutdown closer; he sometimes made things interesting. He was not a guy who would go out there, blow away three batters, and call it a day. There always seemed to be a walk or a hit (or both) before he wiggled his way out of there.

Tigers relief pitcher Jose Valverde delivers against the Boston Red Sox during a game in Boston on August 1, 2012. *(AP Photo/Winslow Townson, file)*

His first season in Detroit was decent. He had 26 saves, averaging one strikeout per inning, but he had a mediocre 2:1 strikeout-to-walk ratio. This was a guy who always took the ball. In one July game, he actually threw 60 pitches to nail down a win in Boston. No, it wasn't pretty, but Valverde made the All-Star team, and more often than not, he got the job done—and most of the time, a colorful dance ensued. But Jose was a good guy and a great team-mate; he never meant any harm by his celebrations.

In 2011, Papa Grande couldn't have been any finer. On 49 occasions he came into a save situation, and 49 times he converted. There were times when things got a little dicey, but at the end of the day, you can't do much better than 100 percent.

An interesting off-shoot of the ways team approach the ninth inning is that closers sometimes struggle in non-save situations. This was perhaps the most consistent trait of Valverde's time in Detroit. In his Tigers career, his ERA in save situations was a stellar 1.65. In non-save situations, it was 4.89. It's all about the mindset.

What happened in 2012 was what you'd call a complete system breakdown. Perhaps we should have realized it right on Opening Day when Papa Grande was summoned to protect a 2–0 lead for Justin Verlander against Boston. Tigers fans had to feel pretty confident. After all, the closer had converted 49 straight saves the year before.

Dustin Pedroia got things going with a double, then Adrian Gonzalez lined a single to left. David Ortiz put the Sox on the board with a sacrifice fly. The Tigers still led 2–1. Things seemed to be under control when Valverde mowed down Kevin Youkilis. All that stood between an impressive Opening Day win was Ryan Sweeney…Ryan Sweeney, who had driven in a grand total of 25 runs in 2011…Ryan Sweeney, who would end the 2012 season with 16 RBI.

Valverde fell behind Sweeney, two balls and one strike. Then Papa left one over the plate, and Sweeney drilled it to right for a game-tying RBI triple. So much for perfection, part two.

Thankfully, the Boston bullpen was much worse than Detroit's. Two singles and a hit by pitch loaded the bases, then Austin Jackson ripped a single to left. With that, the Tigers had a win to start their season.

The rest of Valverde's season was passable but not what the Tigers had been accustomed to. Mirroring his team's malaise, Valverde slogged through the summer months but still had 35 saves by the end of the season. Unfortunately for both Valverde and the rest of the squad, Jose's system failure became a total meltdown during the playoffs.

The implosion started in the ALDS against the Oakland Athletics. The Tigers grabbed a 2–0 lead in the best-of-five series and headed west to wrap things up. After losing Game 3, Detroit was still up two games to one with a chance to close things out behind Max Scherzer. The hard-throwing righty did his part, striking out eight while giving up just a single run in 5⅓ innings.

Jim Leyland's mix-and-match strategy with the bullpen was working to perfection. It went from Octavio Dotel to Phil Coke, Al Alburquerque, and Joaquin Benoit, leading up to Papa Grande, who came in with a 3–1 lead.

Three more outs to wrap up the series. But those three outs never came.

Valverde gave it up, and he did it quickly. Single, double, double, and the game was tied at 3–3. Jose got the next two batters but then gave up a first-pitch single to Coco Crisp. The Tigers were heading to Game 5.

A lesser team might have folded after that type of devastating loss, especially after blowing a chance to wrap up the series. Fortunately, the Tigers had a not-so-secret weapon named Justin Verlander who threw a complete game gem in Game 5. The Tigers were in the ALCS for the second straight season, facing the hated New York Yankees.

———

Yankees fans will remember Game 1 of the ALCS because they saw something they had never witnessed before. Captain Derek Jeter was carried off the field after breaking his left ankle. Tigers fans remember it for some unnecessary drama from Papa Grande.

Starting pitcher Doug Fister gutted through 6⅓ scoreless innings despite not having his best stuff. The pinpoint control Tigers fans were accustomed to seeing from Fister was not there, but the 6'8" righty hung in there for 106 pitches without giving up a run.

Detroit had a 4–0 lead heading into the ninth. Valverde came in to close things out and help his team "steal" home-field advantage. No, it wasn't a save situation, but this seemed like a great chance for Jim Leyland to get his closer back on track. Suffice it to say that nobody could have imagined what came next.

Russell Martin led off with a single, but Valverde struck out Jeter to calm everyone down. On an 0–1 pitch, singles hitter Ichiro Suzuki lined a homer to right, and the Tigers lead was split in half at 4–2.

As he had before, Jose came back with a strikeout, getting MVP candidate Robinson Cano swinging. But once again, trouble was lurking. Mark Teixeira battled for an eight-pitch walk, which brought up 40-year-old Raul Ibanez.

Ibanez is regarded as one of the nicest guys in baseball, and after a hot start, he struggled down the stretch of the season, finishing with an average of .240. But none of this mattered as the veteran left fielder turned on a fastball and crushed a two-run homer to right. This was the last meaningful pitch Jose Valverde would throw as a Tiger.

If there's one thing for which Leyland is best known, it's for being loyal to his players. The manager publicly stood by his closer, saying that Valverde would still be a critical piece of winning the World Series. Surely he knew that the team could not trust their closer in a high-pressure spot, but Leyland knew the importance of portraying confidence in his guy.

One man's failure often leads to another man's opportunity. Phil Coke, who had established himself as a solid middle reliever after failing as a starter, became the team's closer. It wasn't always easy with Coke, either, but he got the job done, and the Tigers swept New York in four games.

To me, the Jose Valverde story is the perfect illustration of the importance of confidence. You always hear that if you want to succeed, you need to believe in yourself. There may be no job in sports where confidence is more essential than being a closer. You have to want the ball and want the pressure. When you screw up, you need a quick case of amnesia.

I'm not 100-percent sure what was going on inside Jose Valverde's head, but Papa Grande was an All-Star closer, making $9 million heading into his free-agent year. There was a decent chance the Tigers would have re-signed him for the 2013 season. After his playoff disaster, he struggled just to find a job, not signing until the Tigers brought him back the following April on a minor league deal. He quickly worked his way back to Detroit, but after a strong start, Papa surrendered six home runs over his last eight appearances and had to go back to the minors.

It's amazing the impact a couple of bad weeks can have on one man's career.

All-Star Effort

One of the highlights of the season for all broadcasters, team personnel, and the players is the All-Star break. We've all worked countless hours for the first half (usually a little more than half) of the season. We've had ups, and we've had downs, but one thing is certain—we all look forward to having a few days to recharge our batteries.

The second half of the 2013 season was about six hours away from starting.

The Tigers were opening up the second half in Kansas City. This was convenient for my family because we had traveled to Kansas to see my son, Brett, a member of the Oakland University baseball team, play for his summer team in Kansas. However hot you've heard it gets in Kansas City during the summer…well, it's true.

On a hot and humid 97-degree Friday, I walked out of our air-conditioned hotel in Kansas City and made a beeline straight for the team bus. Nothing was going to stop me from getting back in the air conditioning…or so I thought.

From the corner of my eye, I saw Jim Leyland who, despite the oppressive heat, was sitting on a bench outside the hotel with a look on his face that seemed to be a combination of relief and satisfaction. I guess since he would be spending the rest of the day in the heat, he figured he'd get an early start.

It was the first time I had seen the skipper since he masterfully managed the AL All-Stars to a 3–0 victory three nights before in New York.

"You put on a great show, Skip," I said.

"We really did good, didn't we?" he replied.

Leyland wasn't just referring to the win, which secured home-field advantage for the AL in the World Series. He was also referring to his successfully navigation through one potential minefield after another.

Look, getting to manage the All-Star Game is a huge honor. It means your team played in the World Series the previous season. Plus, when else will you get a chance to manage the very best players in the entire sport? The 2013 game was Leyland's third time as an All-Star manager.

But every year, no matter who's managing, no matter who the fans vote in, there are always snubs. MLB tried to address this a few years ago by (again) increasing the rosters to 34 players. Then it decided that pitchers who started the Sunday before the game are ineligible to play and can be replaced. Still, there's no way to satisfy everyone.

Each team must be represented. It doesn't matter if you're in first place or have the worst record in the major leagues. Then in 2003, MLB commissioner Bud Selig decided that the All-Star Game would decide home-field advantage in the World Series.

In 2013, Leyland knew that could impact the Tigers come October. I'm not saying they would have won the World Series in 2012 had the first two games been at Comerica Park, but in a best-of-seven series, momentum is everything. In the end, Pablo Sandoval hit three home runs in Game 1, and the Tigers never recovered.

One misconception is that the managers pick the reserves. That used to be the case, but now players, coaches, and other managers also select non-starters. The skipper gets to fill out the roster to 33, then the fans get to vote for the last man in. There's no easy way to do all of this.

Once the game starts, most managers try to give every guy a chance to play, except for one pitcher who is the "long man" should the game go into extra innings. In 2013, Leyland also had the unenviable task of figuring out the best way to use Yankees closer Mariano Rivera, who was playing in the last All-Star Game of his legendary career. The game was in New York (although it was Citi Field, not Yankee Stadium), and everyone wanted to see Mo make a dramatic appearance. And again, Leyland was managing for what could be the difference between his team winning and losing the World Series.

It all adds up to a lot of pressure. But Leyland would not tackle the chore unprepared. He pored over statistics, solicited the opinions of every other manager in the league, and spent countless hours trying to get the selections right with his coaches.

Several weeks before the game, I was in Leyland's office with radio voice Dan Dickerson, and the three of us started discussing who would start the game. That selection is up to the manager.

At that point, it seemed pretty obvious. Tigers pitcher Max Scherzer was 13–0 and clearly the hottest pitcher in the game. But the manager has to take into account how many days of rest the starter will have, how he's throwing at that moment, etc.

Around that time, there was a thought that Rivera should start the All-Star Game as a tribute to his legendary career. Most pitchers only throw one inning in the game (the starter usually goes two) anyway, and the emotional impact of having Rivera starting would be much greater than if the National League was ahead 9–0 and he came out for the eighth inning.

"I think I'm going to start Rivera," Leyland told us that day.

I looked at Dickerson, trying to hide my shock and disbelief. It's one thing for somebody to write a column suggesting a crazy idea; it's another to actually see it come to fruition.

"That's a bold move. Are you really going to start him?" I asked.

"No," he chuckled "I'm not going to start him. Are you kidding me? That's a ridiculous idea."

I remember thinking, *Thank God*. I thought it was a hokey idea the minute I heard about the suggestion. Besides, Scherzer was the best pitcher in baseball in the first half of the season, and he deserved the honor.

———

The night itself couldn't have gone much smoother, and just about all of the Tigers contributed.

Leyland had taken some heat for selecting five setup pitchers instead of an extra third baseman, but Toronto's Steve Delebar won the vote for the final spot and pitched in the critical seventh inning of a 2–0 game along with his Blue Jay teammate, Bret Cecil, who was chosen by Leyland.

The highlight of the AL's 3–0 win was without question the bottom of the eighth inning. That's when Jim decided to make his move and bring in Rivera. The greatest closer in baseball history made his name by finishing off games, but Leyland explained his thinking.

"I wasn't going to take the chance that we might lose the lead in the eighth inning and then Rivera doesn't get a chance to pitch. Then what?"

Come hell or high water, Mariano Rivera was going to pitch in this All-Star Game.

What followed is something no baseball fan—whether they love or hate the Yankees—will ever forget.

Mo came out to a standing ovation by not only the fans but both teams, and there was no doubt who they were cheering since no other player took the field. Rivera stood on the mound all alone. To be honest, All-Star Games are normally pretty forgettable, but every once in a while, you get a moment that stays with you. Thanks to Jim Leyland, all baseball fans had one in July 2013.

Culture Shock

My FOX Sports trip to Germany in February 2013 opened my eyes to what it's like to find yourself in a foreign country and unable to speak the local language.

All of us on the trip—the various broadcasters, former players, and the FOX Sports Girls—had it easy because we were traveling with a group, but it made me stop to think what it's like for players born in other countries to come to the United States to chase their dreams of playing Major League Baseball. For some, the language barrier is the least of their hurdles.

In the offseason before the start of the 2013 season, the Tigers signed Royals catcher Brayan Pena as a free agent to back up Alex Avila. On paper, the move barely registered a blip. Pena came with a reputation as a good defender and a .250-ish hitter. He was by all accounts a friendly guy who loves to play the game, and he plays it hard. He had never played in more than 72 games, and he never surpassed three home runs. Still, there isn't a happier guy in the bigs.

Brayan was born in Havana, Cuba, in 1982. The most simple rights that we take for granted, such as the freedom to live and do what we want, were things that the Pena family could only pray for. Brayan realized that his realistic goal was probably to play for the Cuban National team, but he dreamed of coming to the United States and making a better life for himself and his family.

Of course, the only way to get out of Fidel Castro's Cuba is by defecting. Make it over, and you're a free man. That's the good news. The bad news is that you may never see your family again, and you're certainly never coming back home. As Brayan put it succinctly, "For all of the Cuban players, once you leave the country, you can't go back."

And that's all based on being successful in defecting. Thousands of people have died in such attempts, and others have been punished harshly. It's no wonder that there's no situation on the field that makes Brayan nervous. Defecting is as high stakes as it gets. So, as Brayan told me, everything had to be on the down low…and that meant everything.

"I was 16 when I decided to leave Cuba and defected. I didn't even tell my family because I was afraid of the repercussions from the Cuban government."

Fortunately, as a gifted player, Pena and his teammates would travel out of Cuba for tournaments. This would provide the sliver of hope for those chasing freedom. Pena knew he had a chance at the Pan-Am games in Venezuela, but that didn't make saying goodbye any easier.

"We were leaving for a tournament, and I knew that I may not see [my family] again, but I had to keep it to myself. They didn't know of my plans. I recall that was one of the toughest days of my life, when I hugged my mom and hugged my dad and told them, 'I will see you guys in two weeks,' and knowing in my heart that would be impossible because I was ready to defect."

It wasn't like once he defected that he had a job waiting for him. First, he spent about a year in Venezuela and Costa Rica, awaiting the proper paperwork. The next six months were all about workouts while Brayan readied himself for tryout showcases.

In all, it was about 18 months before he actually signed a deal with the Atlanta Braves in November 2000. At the time, Pena didn't speak any English, but upon inking the contract, it became his top priority.

Brayan hoped he would be good enough, but he was also nervous after hearing horror stories about how Americans didn't welcome immigrants.

His professional career began in Danville, West Virginia, on a Braves team that featured future Pirates first baseman/outfielder Garrett Jones. As if playing in a remote part of West Virginia wouldn't be difficult enough for a Cuban defector, not knowing anyone and barely speaking the language made it even more difficult.

"It's especially hard before and after games because you don't have any family to talk to. It's like you are living in a box. But it's part of your development as a player and a person. Every dream has a sacrifice," Brayan said.

His early experiences gave Brayan an understanding for what players go through today.

"Every time that I see an American player in winter ball, they understand what it's like for us to leave our country. When I see them they say, "Man, we really don't know what we have. We take things for granted. We appreciate now what you guys have to go through."

Former Braves executive and current Royals general manager Dayton

David Lough of the Kansas City Royals is tagged out by the Tigers' Brayan Pena as he tries to score in the third inning of a game on Saturday, September 7, 2013, in Kansas City, Missouri. Lough tried to score from third on a fielder's choice. *(AP Photo/ Ed Zurga)*

Moore arranged to have Pena's family join him. It was a delicate balancing act for Brayan—he wanted his family in his new country, but more importantly he wanted them to be safe.

"My destiny that they would come over here with no fear took me 4½ years. It was a long process because I didn't want them to take a raft, a boat, or nothing like that. I knew it would take time, but I wanted them to do it the right way.

"I am so grateful for this country giving me an opportunity. They opened their arms when my country turned its back on me."

Now that Brayan is an established major leaguer, every day is a celebration for Brayan and his family.

"I [have] a beautiful wife, two beautiful kids, two beautiful boys, and my mom, my dad, my brothers, my sister, my grandmother.... They're all American citizens. For them to be in America, for them not to go through what I went through, it made me feel proud."

Learning Pena's story has opened my eyes to what some players have to go through privately while at the same time performing on the field. For most Latin players, Cuban or otherwise, major leagues or minor leagues, adjusting to life in the U.S. is much more challenging than most of us realize.

Weighty Expectations

The first nine years of Justin Verlander's career have been pretty much a storybook. Rookie of the Year, six-time All-Star (including starting pitcher in 2012), two World Series, and two no-hitters. For a guy who was drafted out of college as the second overall draft pick, things have certainly gone according to plan.

Even in his third full season, when his record fell to 11–17, JV came back with 19 wins the following campaign and finished third in the Cy Young voting. In other words, this guy is beyond good.

Everything came together even better than Verlander could have ever hoped in the 2011 season. He went 24–5, won the Cy Young Award unanimously, and became the first starting pitcher to win the Cy Young and MVP voting in the same season in 25 years.

But one thing about Justin Verlander is that he's never satisfied. He always wants more.

In all likelihood, he's never going to surpass the Cy Young–MVP double—it was truly a once-in-a-lifetime type of season. But that doesn't mean he's not going to try.

The pressure was squarely on JV during the 2012 season. He was coming off a career season, and he was trying to set himself up for the biggest contract he'd ever see, After losing to Texas in the ALCS in 2011, the Tigers were locked and loaded for a run at the World Series.

Justin came out of the gates on fire, winning five of his first six decisions. By the end of June, he was 8–5 with an ERA of 2.69. He was pitching like what he was—the best pitcher in baseball.

Yet before his next start, a media member from another team stopped by our booth and asked, "What's wrong with Verlander?"

I wasn't really ready for this question. "What do you mean?"

"Well, he's lost five games already. He lost five all of last season."

The point of the story is that sometimes we all set the bar so high that we lose sight of what constitutes realistic expectations and what doesn't. It's like we forget that these guys are human. I've never done an actual study on this, but if you look at most players, their numbers at the end of any season are within 10–15 percent of their career lines. There might be a surge, or there might be a dip, but most of the time, they're pretty close to their average.

In 2013, Verlander truly did have an "off" year—not as bad as 11–17, but he was clearly not the same pitcher, going 14–13 with an ERA of 3.46.

Baseball history is littered with pitchers, some of them truly great, who have abnormal declines in performance for no obvious reason.

Consider Cliff Lee, who was demoted to Triple A in 2007, missing the Indians' run to within a game of the World Series. In 2008, the lefty was 22–3, cruising to the Cy Young Award. The next year he fell to 14–13. Lee hasn't won another Cy Young, but he has been one of baseball's best pitchers during his career.

Roger Clemens was Verlander's predecessor in some ways. Clemens was a tall, strong pitcher who wanted the ball and wouldn't give it up. In 1986, the

Rocket won the MVP and Cy Young. He continued to dominate until late in his Boston career. After signing with Toronto as a 34-year-old, Clemens won back-to-back Cy Youngs and consecutive pitching triple crowns, leading in wins, strikeouts, and ERA. Yet when he was traded to the world champion Yankees, the Rocket fell back to Earth with a 14–10 record and 4.60 ERA.

———

Like I said, it happens to everyone. But what separates great pitchers, like the ones I've mentioned, from the rest is how they bounce back. There are some pitchers, however, who never make it all the way back.

In 2012, the San Francisco Giants swept the Tigers en route to their second World Series in three years. For Tim Lincecum, though, three years must have seemed like a lifetime. "The Freak" was the little engine that could during 2008–09, winning back-to-back Cy Young Awards in just his second and third years in the major leagues. At 5'11" and 170 lbs., he defied physics—like a young Pedro Martinez.

Lincecum was 16–10 in the 2010 season, fronting the Giants pitching staff to the World Series. The Texas Rangers were no match for the little man as he mowed them down for two wins during the five game series.

By the time 2012 rolled around, the aura of Lincecum was gone. The once-superstar was 10–15 with a stunning ERA of 5.18. But you have to say the Freak has guts. Manager Bruce Bochy sent Tim to the bullpen for the playoffs, and he was terrific. Against Detroit, he struck out eight Tigers in just 4⅔ innings.

There may have been a little magic left in the arm, but in 2013, he was subpar again with a very uncertain future.

———

There were times during 2013 when Verlander looked like the vintage Verlander, twice taking no-hitters into the seventh inning. And it wasn't like he wasn't putting forth the effort to improve. JV spent countless hours with pitching coach Jeff Jones, tweaking and refining, hoping to regain his previous dominance. There was some chatter that his velocity was down a tick, but he clearly had more than enough "stuff" to win.

The fans and media may have jumped ship, but when it was all said and done in 2013, Verlander had his seventh straight season of at least 200 innings pitched and his fifth straight year of at least 200 strikeouts. His ERA of 3.46 was more than respectable.

JV may not go 24–5 again, but with his work ethic and his ability, he's a pretty good bet to return to dominance, and I'm sure he's not going to morph into Tim Lincecum.

Announcer Speak

When you spend more than 25 years in a broadcast booth, you tend to collect some go-to phrases that seemingly have an endless shelf life. Baseball has a language all its own, and much of it has traveled up to the announcers booth.

Yet some of these phrases mask what we are really thinking. Here is a list of common descriptions we all use, and what they actually mean. Call it Announcer Speak 101.

> **"He's a good catch-and-throw guy."** Usually uttered during a spring-training telecast when a team brings in a catcher from minor league camp. The true meaning? "We know next to nothing about this guy."

> **"They love his arm."** There's actually more than one meaning for this phrase. The first is the same as, "He's a good catch-and-throw guy," except for pitchers. The second is, "This guy throws really hard, but he has no idea where the heck the ball is going."

> **"The kid can really fly."** He can probably run, but he definitely can't hit.

> **"This guy has massive power."** He usually strikes out three times a game.

"He's showing great leadership skills by walking to the mound to settle down the pitcher." The pitcher can't get anyone out, and the catcher just can't take it anymore, so he comes out to stop the bleeding. In a related story, the pitcher wants the catcher to get away from him.

"Their goal is to play meaningful games in September." They're bad. They have no shot.

"He is in a slump, so he is switching it up by wearing his socks high." Yeah, that's it. You haven't had a hit in two weeks because of your socks.

"That's a rookie mistake." Everyone makes the same mistake, but it's more convenient to blame it on the young kids.

"Ownership has given the manager a vote of confidence." Said manager should start packing his bags.

"He's a veteran who's really been helping the young kids." Because the kid isn't good enough to take his job…yet.

"This team needs a manager who is a disciplinarian." Only because the manager they just fired was a players' manager.

"This team needs a players' manager." Because they just fired a disciplinarian.

"The new manager changed the culture." They finally brought in some good players.

"The manager leaving was a mutual decision." Ownership didn't want him, so he quit before he got fired.

CHAPTER 10
CHASING THE PRIZE

After getting swept out of the 2012 World Series by San Francisco, the Tigers set their sights on finishing the job in 2013. General manager David Dombrowski wasted no time adding talent to an already loaded roster.

Less than three weeks after the Fall Classic, Dombrowski made a quick, decisive move, signing free agent outfielder Torii Hunter to a two-year deal. The nine-time Gold Glove player had moved from center field to right later in his career but was considered one of the biggest prizes available, and he would shore up a major hole in the Tigers' defense. With Hunter and the return of designated hitter Victor Martinez from knee surgery, Jim Leyland's team was locked and loaded for a championship.

To whom much is given, much is expected, and the 2013 Tigers were no different. The regular season was to be a rehearsal for the playoffs, but somebody forgot to tell the Indians and Royals. Kansas City put a decent scare into the two-time defending Central champs, but it was Cleveland, with new manager Terry Francona, that rode a 10-game winning streak to close out the regular season and clinch a stunning Wild Card berth, just one game behind the Tigers.

For the second year in a row, Detroit would take on the Oakland A's in the American League Division Series. Oakland was 2012's Cinderella, with a collection of long-haired, low-salaried misfits who won the Western Division. They weren't supposed to be able to repeat their success, but there they were, champions again, with a better record than the highly heralded Tigers.

Just as it had during the season, Detroit would ride its starting pitching. Max Scherzer, a 21-game winner, led a star-studded rotation that also included former Cy Young Award/MVP winner Justin Verlander, ERA champion Anibal Sanchez, reliable Doug Fister, and the rapidly improving Rick Porcello.

In Game 1, the formula worked perfectly; the Tigers scored three runs in the first, Scherzer struck out 11 in seven innings, and Joaquin Benoit struck out the side in the ninth. Detroit was on its way.

But Oakland wouldn't go away and eventually carved out a 2–1 lead in the best-of-five series.

Doug Fister gutted out six tough innings in Game 4 but was out of gas after 104 pitches. Facing elimination, Jim Leyland pushed all the chips to the

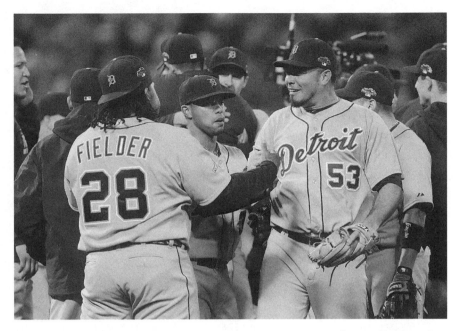

Pitcher Joaquin Benoit (53) is congratulated by teammate Prince Fielder after the Tigers beat the Oakland Athletics 3–0 to win Game 5 of the ALDS in Oakland, California, on Thursday, October 10, 2013. *(AP Photo/Ben Margot)*

center of the table and brought Scherzer out of the bullpen for the first time all year.

The eventual Cy Young winner didn't disappoint. With the bases loaded in the eighth, Max struck out Josh Reddick and Stephen Vogt, then he got pinch hitter Alberto Callaspo to line out, and the threat was over. Scherzer has never been one to hide his emotions, and that night was no different. He stormed to the dugout, violently high-fiving his teammates.

"It was surreal, but that's the stuff you dream about," he said after his series-saving performance.

As tremendous as it was, Max's performance only guaranteed a trip to Oakland for a Game 5 for the second straight season.

Justin Verlander had an up-and-down 2013. This was the first time since early in his career that he wasn't considered the team's No. 1 starter. But none of this mattered on October 10.

JV had shut down the A's in the exact same situation the previous year with a dominating four-hit shutout. That was great. But like the song say, "You ain't seen nothing yet."

Verlander didn't allow a hit until the seventh inning, allowing only two singles through eight, and the Tigers advanced again to the ALCS. I wouldn't be surprised if the California National Guard doesn't let JV past city lines in 2014.

———

The Tigers dramatic win set up what looked like a classic American League Championship Series with the Boston Red Sox. While Detroit expected to reach this point, Boston had completed one of the biggest turnarounds in major league history, going from a last-place season with just 69 wins to 97 wins and the AL East championship.

The Red Sox had good starting pitching, but they weren't quite up to the level of Detroit. Their offense was very good, but they didn't have anyone to

Boston Police officer Steve Horgan celebrates as the Detroit Tigers' Torii Hunter falls over the right field fence into the bullpen trying to catch a grand slam hit by the Boston Red Sox's David Ortiz during Game 2 of the ALCS on Sunday, October 13, 2013, in Boston. *(AP Photo/Charlie Riedel)*

compare with Prince Fielder and Miguel Cabrera. They did, however, have home-field advantage, which at Fenway Park is a significant factor.

Game 1 was really one of the weirdest playoff games I have ever seen. Anibal Sanchez threw six hitless innings with 12 strikeouts. Unfortunately, he also walked six batters and threw 116 pitches, which forced him out of the game.

The Tigers bullpen did the job, refusing to give up a hit until Daniel Nava's single with one out in the ninth. What was even stranger than a near combined no-hitter was that once Nava singled, the Sox were just one swing away from winning the game. But Joaquin Benoit closed the door, and Detroit was three wins away from a return to the World Series.

As impressive as Sanchez was in Game 1, Scherzer took it to the next level in Game 2. Incredibly, Max held the Sox hitless for the first 5⅔ innings, the third straight game that Tigers pitchers had accomplished that feat. Scherzer was absolutely filthy with 13 strikeouts over seven innings. Between the intensity and the high number of strikeouts, Max told Jim Leyland that he was spent after 108 pitches. But the Tigers had a seemingly insurmountable 5–1 lead, so there were no worries. Detroit was a mere six outs away from a commanding 2–0 series lead, and they would be heading back to Comerica Park for three games.

Unfortunately, a not-so-funny thing happened on the way home, and it changed the fates of two franchises and a potential Hall of Fame manager.

Jose Veras relieved Scherzer to start the eighth inning. With one out, Veras gave up a double to Will Middlebrooks. Dependable lefty Drew Smyly came in but walked Jacoby Ellsbury on a full count. Al Alburquerque struck out Shane Victorino before giving up a single to Dustin Pedroia. Now the bases were loaded, there were two outs, and Leyland had a decision to make.

Phil Coke was a playoff hero in 2012 but simply couldn't get anyone out in 2013. The lefty wasn't even on the roster for the Oakland series but was added for the ALCS, and the reason seemed obvious—David Ortiz. Ortiz has always been pretty effective, even against left-handers. But against Coke, Big Papi had no chance with just two hits in 18 at-bats.

Stunningly, the Tigers manager eschewed Coke and called on his closer, Joaquin Benoit, for a four-out save. Count a certain analyst among the most surprised.

Craig Monroe couldn't believe what he was seeing, either. As we watched in the studio, Craig wondered why Coke was not being used in this matchup.

"Papi's had no success against Coke," Monroe said.

Still, the decision had been made, and it didn't take long for the verdict to come in.

Benoit threw an 85-mph change-up right down the middle of the plate, and Papi launched an absolute missile toward right field. Torii Hunter gave it everything he had but flipped head first into the Red Sox bullpen. Papi hit a grand slam and, just like that, the game was tied at 5–5.

In the studio, we looked at each other in stunned silence. It seemed like a bad dream. Scherzer had absolutely dominated the Red Sox, but in one pitch, the series had done an about-face.

"What the hell just happened?" I muttered, still not believing what I had just witnessed. All I could think of at the moment was the late Jack Buck's famous line after Kirk Gibson homered off Dennis Eckersley in Game 1 of the 1988 World Series: "I don't believe what I just saw."

The blast tied the game, but in reality it felt like the Tigers were cooked. In the bottom of the ninth, Johnny Gomes hit a foul pop down the first-base line. Prince Fielder chased it down and dropped it into the crowd. With his second chance, Gomes hit a ball deep into the hole at shortstop. Jose Iglesias made a wild throw that Fielder was unable to block, and Gomes was suddenly on second with no one out.

Tigers starter-turned-reliever Rick Porcello then uncorked a wild pitch, and the winning run was just 90' away. Two pitches later, Jarrod Saltalamacchia ripped it past Miguel Cabrera. And again, just like that, the game was over and the series tied. The Red Sox were back in the series, and the Tigers had to find a way to turn the page.

The series resumed in Detroit, and the Tigers pitching dominance picked up right where it left off. Game 3 was yet another stress fest as Justin Verlander and John Lackey hooked up in a scoreless duel through six innings. Verlander continued his postseason renaissance with eight strikeouts heading into the seventh inning. That's when Mike Napoli crushed a 3–2 pitch over the center-field wall, and Boston had a 1–0 lead.

Red Sox veteran John Lackey had confounded Detroit with 6⅔ scoreless innings, but now the Tigers were into the bullpen.

This can't be the only run of the game, I thought.

I was wrong. Verlander would finish with 10 strikeouts over eight innings, but one swing of the bat had given Boston a 1–0 lead, the eventual win, and a surprising 2–1 lead in the series.

The Tigers offense finally came alive in Game 4 as Detroit pounded a wild Jake Peavy in a five-run second inning and cruised to a 7–3 win behind Doug Fister to even the series at 2–2.

Game 5 is always pivotal in the postseason. The winner on this night would be one win away from the World Series. Anibal Sanchez and Jon Lester were to hook up in a rematch of their classic (albeit weird) Game 1 matchup. There was some question whether the game would be played as rain poured down on Detroit all day long. Neither team was able to take batting practice. Unfortunately for Tigers fans, the Red Sox didn't need it.

It was Detroit who actually had the first scoring chance. With two men on in the first inning, Jhonny Peralta ripped a shot to left field. Cabrera ran through a late stop sign by third base coach Tom Brookens and was out at the plate by 5'.

Boston took advantage, putting up a three-spot in the second and another in the third, jumping out to a 4–0 lead. The Tigers chipped away scoring runs in the fifth, sixth, and seventh innings. However, while the Detroit bullpen had its struggles, Junichi Tazawa and Craig Breslow provided a dependable bridge to closer Koji Uehara time and time again. On this night, Uehara closed it down with a five-out save, and the Red Sox needed just one more win.

That was the bad news for the Tigers. The good news, however, was that they had Scherzer and Verlander, arguably the best 1-2 combo in baseball, slated to start. There was good reason for the Tiger faithful to still feel confident.

The 2013 Cy Young winner didn't disappoint. While not as sharp as he was in his first start, Scherzer allowed only a single run through the first five innings. That's when Boston manager John Farrell committed perhaps his only mistake of the series.

Clay Buchholz was tiring in the sixth, but instead of going with one of his big-three relievers, he called on lefty Franklin Morales to face Victor

Martinez. Big mistake. Victor ripped a single off the left-field wall, and the Tigers had a 2–1 lead. In the studio, we felt like maybe this was the break we had been waiting for.

Prince Fielder had an awful postseason. From dropping a foul ball in Game 2 to his inability to come up with a clutch hit, this was an October to forget for the Tigers big first baseman. But what happened in that sixth inning would haunt Prince for a while.

With one out and men on the corners, Peralta grounded to second. Dustin Pedroia tagged Martinez for the force-out, then he noticed Fielder stuck in no-man's land between third and home. Boston catcher Saltalamacchia chased him down and fell on Prince for the out. Alex Avila struck out, and the rally was over. The Tigers led 2–1, but could have (should have) had more.

One thing everyone learned about this Red Sox team is that they never quit. In the seventh, a double, a walk, and then an error by sure-handed Iglesias loaded the bases.

In the studio, Rod, Craig, and I began to squirm. This didn't feel good.

Then Jose Veras replaced Drew Smyly with Shane Victorino due up, and I felt confident the Tigers could wiggle out of the jam. Being the ever-accurate prognosticator, I offered up the following: "Veras has a good curve, and Victorino hasn't been able to hit a breaking ball in this series to save his life."

Sure enough, Veras got ahead in the count 0–2 on a couple of knee-buckling curves. I was feeling pretty smart.

"Throw him another one, and let's get out of this," I said.

"Be careful—if you throw it, don't hang it," Rod said.

"He won't," I said.

But he did, and Victorino hit it. The ball went over the Green Monster for the series' second stunning grand slam.

I looked at Rod in disbelief. "I can't believe you just called that."

Rod had no response. Neither did Craig. He was in shock, just like the rest of us. For three guys with as much to say as we usually do, you could literally hear a pin drop.

We've watched a lot of baseball, and you know when a team is done. We were done, and so were the 2013 Tigers.

The Final Exit

What the 2013 Tigers achieved was, by most measures, a successful campaign—a third straight Central Division title, a victory against Oakland in the playoffs, and a hard-fought battle in the ALCS. But this team was built to win…and by win, I mean the World Series.

As Shane Victorino's grand slam soared into the Boston night, little did anyone know the seismic shift that was about to happen in the Tigers family. Yes, they were eliminated from the postseason and yes, it was time to start thinking about next year. But only two members of the organization knew they'd be looking for a new manager.

Moments after the devastating Game 6 defeat, Jim Leyland broke it to his team—he was stepping down as Tigers manager. The 69-year-old skipper was tired after 22 seasons, three pennants, and one World Series title.

We all knew that Leyland's career was closer to the end than the beginning, but nobody expected it this quickly. The decision took me by surprise, especially based on a conversation I had with him the previous season.

In mid-May, I slipped into the Starbucks at the team hotel for a cup of coffee and to take care of some game prep for that night's Tigers-Rangers game in Arlington, Texas.

I pulled up a chair at a corner table to work on some player bios when Leyland strolled in wearing a pressed white dress shirt and jeans. The rigors of the season will wear down the best of us, but on this day, the skipper looked fresh and ready for the start of a series against the Rangers.

Leyland pulled up a chair and chatted for a half hour, mostly about the team. The Tigers had just taken two out of three from the Astros, and that night the Tigers-Rangers series opener would feature Yu Darvish against Justin Verlander. However, despite that night's heavyweight matchup, the conversation shifted to Leyland's future.

In retrospect, it was a personal question that perhaps I should not have asked, but it was a casual setting and I asked it anyway.

"How much thought have you given to how much longer you want to do this?" I asked.

"I still feel good," Leyland said. "I have a lot of energy and would maybe like to go a few more years."

It made sense, too. The Tigers were loaded with talent, and their best players were under contract through at least 2014. They had a great owner who desperately wanted to win and would spend whatever it took to accomplish that. For a manager who has a chance to get inducted into the Hall of Fame, a second World Series championship would go a long way.

That conversation in mid-May took on a much different tone on September 7 when Leyland met with GM Dave Dombrowski. Just the night before, the Tigers had blasted the Royals 16–2 in Kansas City.

According to Leyland, "I told Dave, 'I don't know what your plans are, but I will no longer be the manager of the Tigers.'" The Tigers president and general manager was surprised. He had hired Leyland twice and had given no indication that the skipper's job was in trouble.

As I said earlier, players, coaches, and everyone who travels with a big-league team are spoiled. We travel on a team charter, get served the best food, and stay in five-star hotels. But it is still a lot of travel, especially for a manager approaching 70 years of age.

"I could see it coming. The road trips were starting to get long; the fuel was starting to get low," Leyland said.

Even with his energy decreasing, Jim didn't want any distractions for his team. To that end, he told three people about his plans—his wife, Katie; bench coach Gene Lamont; and longtime friend Tony La Russa, who had retired two years earlier after leading the Cardinals to the world championship.

When I think about how prevalent the media is—whether it's newspapers, TV, Twitter, or Facebook—the fact that such a high-profile manager as Leyland could keep this a secret for so long is just amazing.

There's no question that his tenure in Detroit was a successful one. No, he never won the World Series with the Tigers, and that gnawed at him. Because of this, not everyone was in his corner. Leyland had many critics along with his fans.

The facts bear it out. In 2003, the Tigers tied an American League record with 119 losses. Three years later, they were in the World Series. From 2011 to 2013, Leyland took his team in the playoffs three straight years for the first time since 1907–09.

Jim Leyland summed it up better than anyone. "I came here to change talent to team, and I think with the help of this entire organization, I think we've done that. We've won quite a bit. I'm very grateful to have been a small part of that."

Timing Is Everything

The memory is still fresh in my mind. Kenny Lofton's fly ball to center is squeezed by Darin Erstad, and the 2002 World Series is over. In Anaheim, California, the Angels and their fans celebrate their first World Series title. More than 2,000 miles away in Michigan, I sit in my new home, taking in the celebration on TV and feeling both excited and sad at the same moment.

I had left the Angels following the 2001 season to take a job in my hometown, covering my favorite childhood team. That was a once-in-a-lifetime opportunity. Still, the year after I leave, the Angels win it all. Timing is not my strong suit.

I would be lying if I said I didn't question that career move, but only because I had lost out on broadcasting a World Series winner and didn't know if that would ever present itself again.

Twelve years later, I wouldn't change a thing. The Tigers suffered through more than a decade of losing baseball when I arrived in Detroit in 2002. And in my first few years back, things actually got worse. The year 2003 provided 119 losses, and the culture hadn't changed much at that point.

However, what I have witnessed the last eight years with Jim Leyland at the helm easily qualifies as the best stretch of baseball in Tigers history—a history that spans more than 100 years. For that, I constantly remind myself how some bad timing in 2002 turned into the best career move of my life.

No, the Tigers haven't matched the Angels title of 2002, but that doesn't tell the whole story. I have been at the mic for a team that has four postseason appearances, three straight Central Division titles, and two AL pennants in the last eight years.

I've had the great fortune of calling two Justin Verlander no-hitters (and several other games that came close) and his MVP/Cy Young double dip. I witnessed Miguel Cabrera's Triple Crown season, the first in baseball since 1967. I've spent countless hours talking to—no, learning from—one of the best managers of our generation in Jim Leyland. And I did all of this from the best seat in house in the greatest baseball town in America.

I remember the feeling I had in 1984 as a fan when the Tigers last won a World Series title. I can't wait to experience the same feeling from the booth.

Detroit will always be a baseball town, and I can't believe that I've had a front-row seat for some of the best moments in its deep, rich history. If only these walls could talk....

SOURCES

Books

Bosco, Joseph A. *The Boys Who Would be Cubs: A Year in the Heart of Baseball's Minor Leagues*. New York: William Morrow & Co., 1990.

Websites

ESPN.com

Foxsports.com

www.baseball-reference.com

www.hauntedrooms.com

www.stats.com.

ABOUT THE AUTHORS

Mario Impemba is the Detroit Tigers' Emmy Award–winning play-by-play announcer on FOX Sports Detroit. A native of Detroit, Impemba was named the 2011 Michigan Sportscaster of the Year by the National Sportscasters and Sportswriters Association.

After spending eight years broadcasting in the minor leagues (in Peoria, Illinois; Davenport, Iowa; and Tucson, Arizona), Impemba landed his first major league job as the radio play-by-play voice of the Los Angeles Angels in 1995. Following seven seasons in Southern California, he returned to his hometown as the TV voice of the Detroit Tigers in 2002.

Impemba is a graduate of Michigan State University, receiving his B.A. Degree in Telecommunication in 1985.

Mike Isenberg is a multiple Emmy Award–winning coordinating producer at FOX Sports Detroit. Prior to coming Michigan, Isenberg spent six-plus years as a sportscaster in Elmira, New York, and Scranton, Pennsylvania, followed by 10 years at ESPN. *If These Walls Could Talk: Detroit Tigers* is his second book. *The Longest Year: One Family's Journey of Life, Death and Love* (www.thelongestyearbook.com) was published in 2009.

Isenberg grew up in Sudbury, Massachusetts, as a huge Red Sox fan, but he has worked with Impemba, covering the Tigers, since 2006.